Fell's Guide to

DOUBLING THE PERFORMANCE

OF YOUR CAR

FELL'S GUIDE TO

DOUBLING THE PERFORMANCE

OF YOUR CAR

by

WILLIAM HAMPTON

INTRODUCTION AND TROUBLE-SHOOTER CHARTS

by

BILL TAKAS

Former Race Car Driver
Regional Champion, Sports Car Club of America

Illustrated

FREDERICK FELL PUBLISHERS, INC., NEW YORK

Library of Congress Cataloging In Publication Data

Hampton, William.
    Fell's guide to doubling the performance of
your car.

    1. Automobiles--Maintenance and repair. I. Ti-
tle. II. Title: Doubling the performance of your
car.
TL152.H32 1977   629.28'8'22   77-2978
ISBN 0-8119-0267-6
ISBN 0-88391-053-5 pbk.

Copyright © 1977, William Hamptom

For information address:
Frederick Fell Publishers, Inc.
386 Park Avenue South
New York, New York 10016

Published simultaneously in Canada by:
Thomas Nelson & Sons, Limited
Don Mills, Ontario, Canada

MANUFACTURED IN THE UNITED STATES OF AMERICA

1 2 3 4 5 6 7 8 9 0

TABLE OF CONTENTS

INTRODUCTION

Bill Hampton's book FELL'S GUIDE TO DOUBLING THE PERFORMANCE OF YOUR CAR has brought back to mind all the bent, broken, wheezing and whimpering, chugging and clunking cars that have been in my life as long as I can remember. Because my father had a fairly busy automobile repair shop, I was able to see and hear the changes that those great machines were put through. I didn't understand how it was done, but it was easy enough to recognize a car being towed in on the back of the truck, the mechanic unable to start it, going under the hood, unscrewing something, looking at it, getting some little bits and pieces from the parts room, fussing around some more, trying the key, Hey, it starts! But it still has a shake. My father would then come over and, reaching under the hood, would gently touch something and the big car would begin to purr.

I got hooked early.

Since then I've spent thousands of hours trying to duplicate that touch on an engine.

There's a lot of satisfaction in using tools, in solving riddles, in making something new again or even making it better than new. All this can be done with little or no expense.

Bill Hampton has written the kind of book that allows you, the layperson, to get hooked too. Understanding your car helps you to operate it more confidently, more smoothly and therefore, more safely and more reliably. There is a sense of freedom in being mobile and also knowing exactly how the whole machine works.

But there is also another dimension to having a car. In so many ways today our life style is based on having personal transportation, an automobile. Shopping centers have been built outside the cities and towns. Streets, highways and expressways make it possible for you to commute to a job that would be virtually inaccessible if you had to use public transit. Towns and suburbs have grown up with no public transit. All this makes your car a necessity. and reliability is the first quality necessary in that car.

It used to be fairly easy and inexpensive to maintain a car for a couple of years, then trade it in for a newer one. Now, in the past couple of years the unstable economy (not just in the United States, but throughout the world) and the government mandated safety and emission requirements have brought us to the point where the costs involved in owning a car (purchase price, insurance, mechanic rates, parts) have doubled. Unfortunately, your income has not.

But you still need your car. If you re-think your attitude toward your machine you'll find there are ways to bring its expense right back down to a level that will fit a lot more comfortably into your budget. Aside from not trading it as often, doing your own maintenance is the simplest and surest way of saving. And, if you establish a regular maintenance schedule, you'll probably make your car more reliable than in the past. This can lead to even more saving. Towing was always expensive.

Basic maintenance is primarily looking at things. It's not hard work and really doesn't take a lot of time. In this book Bill Hampton tells you not only where and when to look, but what to look for, He goes on to tell you what to do if what you find is not right. Even if you find something wrong that you feel you cannot handle, the information here will help you to describe it more accurately to your mechanic, so he doesn't have to spend time (which you pay for) finding the malfunction.

All in all, you should find FELL'S GUIDE TO DOUBLING THE PERFOR-MANCE OF YOUR CAR an easy, instructive way to help you keep your car running well. You will learn to operate it more efficiently, make it last longer, save a lot of money, and hopefully have some fun from enjoying a job well done. Dig in...

Bill Takas
Former Race Car Driver
Regional Champion, Sports Car Club of America
Member: Porsche Club of America
　　　　　Sports Car Club of America

HOW TO USE THIS BOOK

Everyone who drives will benefit from this book. The information, illustrations and charts have been selected to cover both day-to-day automobile problems and long-range maintenance.

PART I—PERFORMANCE BUYING was designed for the potential car buyer, or, for those of you looking for a trade-in. *Your Car And Its Meaning To You* gets right down to the position your car plays in your life—from weekend entertainment to full-time necessity. *How To Buy The Right Car For You* covers the possible purposes and reasons you may be entertaining for buying a car—your personal needs and specifications. *How To Buy A New Car* will give you insights into price discussions, bargaining and the accessories you may or may not need which keep the total cost going up. *How To Buy A Used Car* highlights both the best reasons for buying from a private seller as well as the best reasons for buying from a dealer. It discusses guarantees, how to evaluate a used car, what to look for, what to check out before making that final decision.

PART II — THE CHARTS. This section was created for easy access to your MOST IMMEDIATE problems. If you are spending a lot of money on fuel, the lead-off chapter, *How To Double Your Gas Mileage* gives you very important tips on acceleration, braking, miles per hour, the size of your car versus its fuel appetite, and how to cut gas station costs.

THE TROUBLE-SHOOTER CHARTS should be kept close to the driver's seat. If you slide into the seat and your ignition won't turn over, turn to the WHEN YOUR CAR WON'T START TROUBLE-SHOOTER or IGNITION TROUBLE—SHOOTER. If you're driving down a highway and hear a ping, a thud, a thump, or any other noise, take a look at the NOISE TROUBLE-SHOOTER. There are eight

TROUBLE-SHOOTER CHARTS for you to examine. Each offers a Symptom-Cause-Remedy checklist, written in language accessible to the layperson as well as your mechanic.

PART III - PERFORMANCE MAINTENANCE AND DRIVING was designed to give you more specific information about the various facets of car maintenance. How each system in your car works, how it can be cared for to keep it in top running condition, and how the mechanism works, are all provided. If you're worried about what you'll need to begin, *The Tools You'll Need* gives you a descriptive and illustrative sample of what to use or what to buy.

Starting with the simpler systems, *Your Tires, Your Brakes, Your Fuel System*, PART III works up to the more complex systems, *Your Electrical System, Your Ignition System, Your Steering and Suspension, Lubrication*. Each chapter has been written to allow you to approach a particular system with both a knowledge of its functions, and a photographic guide to its particular anatomy.

Performance Driving offers you the safest, most efficient, and comfortable tips to city or country driving.

PART IV - THE GLOSSARY is an unusual and most efficient section. It has been illustrated for more immediate recognition of some mechanical parts and terms. Use it to better understand the language of your mechanic, automobile dealer or parts seller.

We wish you safe and trouble-free motoring.

Bill Takas, Regional Champion, Sports Car Club of America

Part I
PERFORMANCE BUYING

Chapter 1

YOUR CAR AND ITS MEANING TO YOU

Have you ever given any serious thought to what your car means to you?

Can you imagine what it would be like not to have it?

Take a moment to ponder that question. If you're like millions of other auto owners who depend on their cars for daily transportation you may find it difficult to imagine not having a steering wheel to slide behind.

After all, for many of us the automobile is such an integral part of our lives that we usually take it for granted. Like many other things in our lives, we fail to truly appreciate the four-wheeler until something goes wrong with it.

My purpose here is to give you an in-perspective view of the auto as a marvelous mechanical mode of transportation.

It seems that the automobile is continually maligned by certain groups as being a threat to the welfare of society in the sense that it causes considerable death and injury on our roads. And, there are other ecology-minded parties who view the auto as a significant danger to our environment.

It's true that automobiles have proven to be dangerous when mishandled, and they do emit certain pollutants which certainly don't do the environment any good.

But, let's look at these two facts in perspective: first of all, in most cases, the human element is the reason for accidents. Carelessness, on someone's part, turns the

3

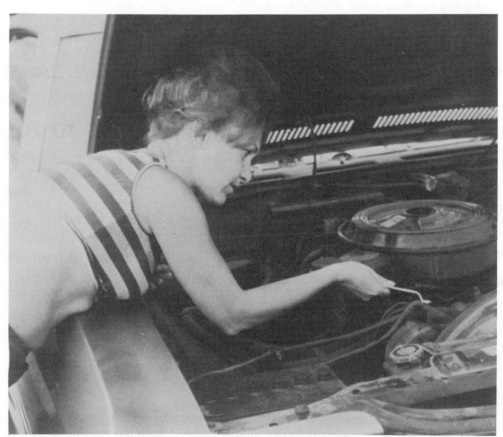

You don't have to be a master mechanic to improve your car's performance. But you do need a basic knowledge of what makes a car work, along with a little patience. Even if you've never so much as looked under the hood of a car before, you can learn to do many forms of maintenance to keep your car running well.

automobile from a docile, obedient servant into a lethal weapon. It has no evil intent of its own to hurt anyone. It merely responds to the behavior of its operator.

As far as polluting the air, the auto doesn't emit as much carbon monoxide as Nature's vegetation does, and our technologists are presently finding ways to reduce it.

This book can help you minimize your chances of becoming involved in an accident, and at the same time help to reduce the pollution your car contributes to the environment.

How?

For one, if you keep your car crisply tuned and functioning the way it was intended, you'll stand a better chance of avoiding an accident. Suppose you have to suddenly accelerate in a very short distance. If your car bucks and sputters, it can't get out of the way quickly enough. Should you have to stop quickly and your brakes are worn too much, guess what happens?

Because of the higher cost of everything and less money to spend, you may not want to trade in your car as frequently as you used to. The longer you have it, the less the annual depreciation. And, though your car may need a little more tending to, the cost may be even less by "doing-it-yourself." Also, if you depend on your car for work transportation, you're making an important investment in your earning ability— an investment of maybe just minutes in a week.

Don't dread the idea of having to work on something just because you don't understand it, *now*.

Let this book help you get that understanding.

It's designed for the car owner who knows little or nothing about the workings of his vehicle. All that this book really demands is that you exercise a little patience and common sense along with your ability to interpret everyday words to unravel the "gizmos and whatchamacallits" that make up an automobile.

By starting out with the simplest maintenance jobs, you'll find your skill and confidence increasing to where you'll be doing things which you never thought yourself capable.

A few words of caution, though: don't get carried away and perform something you don't understand. For example, replacing a fuel-line filter is one thing; but tearing apart a carburetor is something else. Use your common sense as to how far you can go.

There's a lot of satisfaction in being a "shade tree" mechanic; but one step at a time.

Let this book take you by the hand to show you the basics of your car.

5

When you're shopping for an older used car, get down and look underneath the car for a severely rusted frame. If it looks like this, forget the car.

Chapter 2

HOW TO BUY THE RIGHT CAR FOR YOU

Unless you know exactly what you want in a car—and money is no object—buying the right car for you can be a little exasperating to say the least.

There are so many factors to consider; what size car, what size engine, should it have air conditioning, automatic transmission, power steering, reclining seats, automatic back scratcher, options ad infinitum. Although an automatic back scratcher isn't an available option (as yet), you'll still find many other accessories to tempt you and to strain your pocketbook.

So, you have to sit down and do a little logical thinking, before you throw reason to the wind and excitedly scrawl your name on the bill of sale for that mass of shiny metal in the showroom.

Put that new car brochure aside for now, and read these next few pages; maybe they'll help you pick out a car.

SPECIFICATIONS

To be of much help here, I'll have to define some terms and clarify some ideas about size. Compact, sub-compact, intermediate and full-sized are terms that loosely refer to different sized cars. Some people relate them to the length of a car, others relate them to the weight. About the only time the length of a car is important is when you're trying to park it and it's easy to measure. I'm going to relate these terms to weight because at speeds under 70 MPH the weight you're trying to move has much more bearing on gas mileage than just about any other dimension. So full-size will mean 4,000 lbs. and over; intermediate means 3,000 to 4,000 lbs.; compact means a car weighing between 2,000 and 3,000 lbs.; sub-compact means under 2,000 lbs. This dimension is harder to measure, but easy to find in the owner's manual or sales brochures.

Let's clarify here what a big or small engine is. Some people have the erroneous idea that the number of cylinders makes an engine large or small. Not so. Cubic inches or litres is the measure. One litre is 61 cubic inches, therefore, a 305 cubic inch V-8 is five litres. A VW Rabbit is 1½ litres. Cars have been built with 8 cylinder engines and 12 cylinder engines and even a 16 cylinder engine (BRM) displacing only one and a half litres. On the other end of the scale there have been 4 cylinder engines displacing 20 litres or more. One litre is slightly more than a quart, so picture each one of those 4 cylinders being 1¼ gallon size!

Now this is all directly related to economy because with every revolution of the engine you fill half of the litres with fuel mixture. Not bad with a 1½ litre engine, but if you have one of the older 7 litre super cars, there's no way you can avoid using more gas short of parking it.

Where the number of cylinders does make a difference is in smoothness. An exaggerated example: a four-litre, 2 cylinder engine would have one half-gallon size explosion every revolution. But, that same four-litre size in an 8 cylinder engine would have 4 pint-size explosions spread around one revolution while still delivering the same power. Much smoother.

The quality of horsepower is determined by the amount of fuel burned in the cylinders in a given time. Horsepower is raised by increasing the amount of fuel pushed through in each revolution and/or increasing the number of revolutions per minute (RPM).

This is simplified, of course, but essentially very correct. Variations in design and to a degree tuning, will make an engine more efficient in utilizing its fuel, but in some ways this makes the exhaust gases dirtier. So all the auto makers have been scramblling in the past few years to think in a new way about what "efficiency" means.

Consider another measure, lbs. per H.P. (pounds per horsepower). These numbers can tell you very quickly what the potential zap of a car is whether it's big or little.

New cars now seem to generally carry over 30 lbs. per H.P. The quicker models carry around 25 lbs. per H.P., and the real swifties are hauling 20 or under. That's not like the old muscle-car days, when you couldn't show your face around the drive-in (or your pipes to anyone) if you had more than 10 lbs. per H.P.

So, basically in any car you consider buying look for the following:

As low a weight as you feel comfortable with—

As low a cubic inch/litre displacement as you can find—

An engine that will give you as low a lbs. per H.P. ratio as you wish. Low displacement with relatively high horsepower means that the engine is a pretty efficient design.

One last note: if you frequently carry heavy loads (six adults, average 900 lbs.) or tow a trailer, count that in your lbs. per H.P. ratio.

Okay, you have some information to work with. Now you have to put yourself into the equation.

NEEDS

Ask yourself, "What is the primary reason for buying this car?" Then ask, "What will this car be mostly used for?" Is this car for driving back and forth to work everyday? Is it a short or long distance? Will there always be a group of people, like a car pool or the kids going to school? Is this the only car? The main car? The second? The third? The Sunday go-to-meeting car? These aren't all the questions, but just examples of the type you should ask. You're a salesman driving hours a day with sample cases full of valuables. You should wonder about the size and shape of the luggage space and how comfortable is the driver's seat. A station wagon might seem logical at first, but maybe it would be much more convenient to be able to stow things out of sight. A large trunk? If you spend hours a day in the car, think about a VERY comfortable seat. A reclinable bucket seat? You drive a lot of miles every week and you don't get paid for the mileage, so miles per gallon is important. A small engine? You also want peppy performance. A light weight car?

Okay. The criteria is this: A quick but economical car with a large, lockable luggage space and a very comfortable driver's seat. This sounds like a compact, or maybe even one of the better sub-compacts. Well, here's a 2 plus 2 Hatchback. It looks

9

good: 25 lbs. per H.P., 30 MPG, reclining bucket seat and a locking panel over the whole luggage area...But what about taking the whole family across town to grandma's every Sunday? You have to spend many hours in that seat. The more comfortable you are, the safer we all are, and the better you'll feel when you're trying to close a sale.

Again, these questions and answers may not apply to you. Maybe you're considering bringing another car into the family. Is your current one still making you happy as your main vehicle? Think about getting a cheap used car if you just need a simple utility machine. (It may also give you more practice in do-it-yourself maintenance.) Or, if your main means of moving is getting tacky and tired, relegate it to utility status, but use it as a model for what your new one will be. How did you use this car? What purpose did it serve best? In what areas was it wrong? Get the idea?

Okay. Onto the next step.

Chapter 3

HOW TO BUY A NEW CAR

If your piggy bank is bulging enough to let you think about a new car, let's see what you should consider.

Today a new car costs double what it did just four years ago. You'd think this would have stopped impulse buying. But no. It still happens that a new car shopper will spot a model that seems so appealing that it's a matter of love at first sight. Without really evaluating the car or comparing it with other models, the impulse buyer thinks that he or she has found the perfect car to drive happily ever after.

And, once in a while it works out. But oftentimes the impulse buyer finds that after only a few weeks or months of ownership, he or she hasn't found the "dream machine" after all.

For one reason or another, he or she decides to trade it in on another car. And here's where such a person loses the proverbial shirt.

The impulse buyer finds that this almost-new car has dropped about a fourth of its value in just a few weeks or months. The impulsive one cannot understand why a new car dealer won't allow more money for this almost-new car.

But turn around and consider the dealer's point of view: If the dealer allowed you almost what you paid for your car new, he'd have to ask a selling price for it that would approximate about what you gave for it originally. And a perspective shopper would think it silly not to spend a few dollars more for a brand new model like yours and have a totally new car with a full warranty.

11

A car depreciates the most during its first year of use.

If you trade every two or three years, the rate of depreciation has slowed compared with the first year, and your loss of value is a bit less each year.

There are all kinds of pros and cons about when to trade. Again, if you can afford it, do what you will. On the other hand, if you can't afford to trade or don't want to, it's possible you could keep your car for several years and get way ahead of the game.

If you learn to do much of your own maintenance, this is the way to go. The money you'd normally put out for car payments can be put into the cookie jar for maintenance of your car and peace of mind.

A small car's biggest advantages are that it will give better economy and more maneuverability than will the big cars. Sub-compact models with four cylinder engines and four-or-five speed transmissions can get anywhere from 25 to 40 miles per gallon.

Which needs do you consider more important?

Once you've established the size of the car you need, next comes the matter of deciding what options, if any, you need.

Start with the engine. As with deciding on a particular size of car, you must carefully consider what size engine you need. You need to select an engine compatible with the size of your car, the loads you plan to haul, and the options you want on your new car.

A 30 lbs. per H.P. engine may be fine in a compact, where you won't be adding much of a load. But you certainly don't want it in a station wagon that will be crammed with a bunch of kids, pets, luggage and a camper on the back. Remember that can raise lbs. per H.P. ratio over 40, and that's sluggish.

For reserve performance, you should get an engine a little on the large size rather than one that just meets your anticipated needs. Although you might be tempted to opt for the smaller engine because it delivers better gas mileage than a little larger engine, just make sure that you don't plan to haul more than the engine can handle or subject it to load conditions it wasn't meant for.

In identical sized cars, a small engine that works hard will deliver less mileage than an engine that "coasts" along. Besides the better mileage, a larger engine that's not under strain will last longer than an overworked small engine.

Depending on the kind of driving you do, you can order optional axle ratios to extract more usable performance from the engine. Although such options like air conditioning, AM/FM stereo radio, and reclining seats are appealing, ask yourself first, "Do I really need them?"

If good gas mileage is your prime consideration, you may want to forgo an automatic transmission. You can gain a couple or so extra miles to the gallon and save yourself anywhere from 300 to 400 dollars in the process. But if you do a lot of urban driving, the convenience of an automatic might outweigh the better economy of the standard transmission. Full-size cars without automatic transmissions are worth slightly less than those with them, when it comes to trading them in.

Power steering should be considered only for a middle to heavy intermediate or full sized car. The power helps only when trying to park a really heavy car.

Another accessory that helps your total-control driving is power brakes. If you plan on getting an intermediate-size or larger car, and want to haul a trailer, power brakes are definitely recommended. If you have a choice between drum and disc brakes, opt for the discs. They cost more, but they provide superior stopping power without the danger of fading when they're hot, or of grabbing when they're applied. Another big plus for disc brakes is that water doesn't reduce their stopping capability.

Another option that adds to your total comfort driving is air conditioning. But it's about the most expensive option you can put on a car, and it makes any repairs much more difficult because the air conditioning components would have to be removed before maintenance can be done on the water pump. Air can drop your miles-per-gallon figure by two or three miles.

But looking at the plus side of the column, air conditioning adds to a trade-in's value, and options like air conditioning, tinted glass, power seats, AM/FM radio, power windows, and reclining seats all add to your total comfort driving.

Most late-model cars are given credit at trade-in time for the following options: automatic transmission, power steering, power brakes, air conditioning, power seats and windows, vinyl roof, special sports and decor packages, and, in the case of some station wagons, a luggage rack.

Right at the top of your list of important options should be good tires. Opt for the steel-belted radial tires. They'll not only outwear conventional tires, but they'll increase your gas mileage and provide your car with sure-footed handling, especially on curves and wet roads.

Top-brand radials are guaranteed 40,000 miles or more, which says something for their durability.

They may cost more, but they're worth the extra cost, for the peace of mind they provide alone.

Once you've decided on the car you want and the options, next comes the little matter of deciding how you're going to pay for it. Although you pay more for a new car

13

than for a used car, you can usually get a lower interest rate and a longer period to pay for it. But over the longer period remember that your interest will be considerably more. Pick the shortest time you can without crippling your budget.

When you've finally decided on the particular model of car, chances are you'll want to shop more than one dealer to get the best price.

If at all possible, try to sell your trade-in privately through classified ads in the newspaper, notes on bulletin boards, and word-of-mouth among acquaintances. By doing this, you have the advantage of getting the salesman to give you a discount on an outright purchase.

Where you get an exceptional deal is on a slow-moving model of which the dealer may be overstocked. In such an instance, the dealer may sell as low as $100.00 to $50.00 over his cost, just to reduce his stock of slow-movers.

You can tell a slow-moving model by the special deals or discounts advertised. If such a car fits your needs, you're in a good bargaining position. However, don't succumb to an attractive price, if the car doesn't fit your needs.

You're better off paying more money for a car that is suitable for your driving needs than getting a so-called bargain that you'll try to trade off in a few months.

And don't ever buy a new car without driving it first. Out on the road a car can give you an entirely different impression from the feeling you get sitting in it in the showroom.

Chapter 4

HOW TO BUY A USED CAR

Okay, let's say that after checking and rechecking your finances, you find that you can't afford a new car.

So, you start thinking about a used car. You start weighing the prospects of buying someone else's troubles versus finding a low-mileage cream-puff at a fraction of a new car's price.

A private seller, who usually advertises in the classifieds or by word of mouth, or a new/used car dealer, either one can be the owner of just the car you're looking for. Sometimes the private owner will sell below average retail; then again, he might ask even more than would a dealer. Most private sellers, as well as dealers, expect some haggling. If you feel the price of a car is too high for the condition it's in, make the seller an offer.

Of course, if the seller has a nice car, priced moderately, he may remain justifiably firm on his price.

When you're shopping for a car, study used-car prices in the newspaper. If you question the price of a used car, regardless of whether it's privately owned or dealer owned, try to find out from another dealer, if possible, what price they have on that same model.

As stated earlier, unless a private seller has an exceptional car priced within reason, he shouldn't expect to get quite the price a dealer would unless he is giving a guarantee.

A dealer, on the other hand, will place a guarantee on all late-model used cars.

15

Depending on the dealer and the car, the guarantee may be 100% warranty for thirty days, which means that if something should go wrong, the dealer absorbs all the costs.

Many dealers use the common thirty-days, fifty/fifty kind of guarantee, in which all costs are split down the middle.

The danger with this warranty is that an unscrupulous dealer could inflate the repair bill, so that your half of it would cover the dealer's costs, too. Hence, the advantage of buying from only a reputable dealer.

How do you tell a reputable dealer? If you inquire around, you'll hear about different dealers by word-of-mouth advertising. Of course, you can't believe everything bad you hear about some dealers, because some buyers who may have felt they were wronged in some way by a certain dealer may not be justified in their complaints. It depends which side of the fence you're on, but there's usually two sides to every story—even in the realm of car sales.

If you ever feel that you have suffered a major wrong by a dealer who sold you a bad vehicle and won't do anything to rectify it, you have every right to contact your Better Business Bureau and Consumer Protection Agency.

When it comes to buying a used car, you don't have the degree of selectivity that you have when buying a new car. With the latter, you can order exactly what you want. In the used-car market, you have to choose from what's available. You'll be lucky indeed to find a car exactly the way you want it; but it does happen.

As with new-car buying, be on guard for impulse-buying a used car just because you can't find what you want right away, or because the price sounds attractive. Keep your feet on the ground and buy according to your needs. Unless you keep this thought foremost in your consciousness, it's easier than you realize to succumb to a sales pitch on a car that really doesn't fit your needs.

A good car salesman can subtly build up the desire in you for a car. He may not pressure you, but he can smooth-talk you into thinking a certain car was just meant for you.

As for the age-range of a used car, you'll find that a two or three-year old car has suffered its worse depreciation. You may be able to pick up a nice low-mileage car in this age-range for about half what it cost new. Although you can find a low-mileage car in good shape that's five, six, seven, or more years old, the odds are against it.

It's false economy to buy an old, high-mileage car in need of major mechanical repairs, unless you can do most of the work yourself.

Only you can decide if a used car, however old, is a good buy for you. Some

16

people can buy a hundred-dollar car and run it for years and put nothing in it. Then they can turn around and sell the car for what they paid for it. That's real value…and no depreciation. But such a car could blow up in six weeks of ownership. So, who can say which way to go.

In any event, there are a few techniques you can employ to evaluate a used car to see if it's a good buy for you.

Let's see what they are.

When you see a car that attracts your attention, one of the first things you do after checking out the year is to look at the odometer mileage.

Like anyone else, you prefer a used car with low mileage. But low mileage isn't always indicative of a car that's in good shape and has lots more miles left in it. The author has seen cars with 60,000, 70,000, or more miles in better condition than cars that had only 20,000 or 30,000 miles.

One doubt you might have when you look at a low-mileage car that's several years old is if the mileage is actual, or if it has been turned back. Not only is it illegal to turn an odometer's mileage back ($10,000 fine if the offender is caught) but newer cars have their speedometer mechanism rigged with a small inking pad that will mark the numbers, if they're turned back.

Should you have any doubts about the mileage reading on a used car, ask the salesman, or private seller (if he's not the original owner) who the previous owner was. In this way you can get verification on the mileage at the time of trade. If you aren't given the name, for some cockeyed reason, forget the car and look elsewhere.

Aside from high mileage, there's nothing that'll detract more from a used car's appearance and value than rust. Once it gets a foothold, it'll spread and eat holes in metal unless it's done away with by metal surgery. A rusted area must be completely eliminated and new metal riveted or welded in place. Quality body and fender work is very expensive. (Quality means straightening or replacing panels, not filling with putty or fiberglass).

But beware of the selling party who just covers up the rust with paint or tapes over the rusted areas. In a short time, the rust pops back out and continues its cancerous spread. You must be on your toes for rust on any used car that you look at. Even one-year old cars can be rusted more than some older cars.

When you're looking that used car over, inspect the areas such as the rocker panels (body panel under the doors) and the edges around the wheelwells. Incipient

17

rust will show itself by blisters in the paint.

Other areas for rust are metal trim strips and the areas around the window sills. Open the trunk and lift up the mat. Rust holes in the trunk floor will admit exhaust fumes into the passenger compartment, as that invisible, odorless carbon monoxide stealthily seeks you out.

Lift up the hood and check for rust on the inside of the fenders. Same goes for around the underside of the doors when you open them and the hinges where they fasten to the body.

Even if you're given a special low price for the car that's severely rusted, you'd better check with a body shop to see just what major body work and painting will cost.

If you're looking at a car several years old and the seller is asking only a few dollars for it, you may feel that it's too good a bargain to pass up. After all, you can always use it for a "fishing or hunting" car, or turn around and sell it for a profit, right?

Maybe! Sometimes that bargain has its frame rusted so badly that one good pot-hole snaps it in two. Old cars should be examined closely on their undersides for weakened frames and suspension members.

If you don't see any rust and the paint looks new for a car several years old, it's probably been repainted. You can tell even the most professional paint job if you look closely enough for tell-tale signs of overspray on the metal trim around the glass. Stand alongside the car and look down the length of it. If it had body work done, you might be able to detect a rippled appearance.

Because a used car is just that—used—you have to check for many possible faults that the new car buyer doesn't have to worry about.

Take the tires: They could reveal any front-end misalignment problems. See if the spare is good.

Worn shocks and sagging springs are other common weaknesses among used cars, especially worn shocks. A sagging spring is obvious: does any corner of the car sit lower than another corner? Either a worn or broken spring would cause that. Push down on one fender and note how the car rebounds. Should the car come up and stop when you let go, the shock is okay. If the car goes up and down a few times before it stops, you have a case of mushy shocks. Worn shocks are a definite hazard to handling.

Try the lights and turn signals. They should all work. If you live in a state that requires inspections, look on the windshield to see if the car has the latest inspection sticker on it. If it's not current, inquire why. Could be the car needs considerable work to pass inspection.

18

Start the engine. Although you have to be really familiar with engines to identify various noises, you can still get an idea if the engine is in decent shape. It shouldn't make any rumbling or knocking sounds which would indicate bad bearings. A clicking sound is common to an engine until the oil has had a chance to circulate.

Squeaking sounds can come from loose fan belts, which isn't all that serious. A rattling sound from the front of the engine could be a bad water pump. If you aren't that familiar with engines, it's a good idea to take along someone who is.

Look at the engine's appearance; is it clean? If it's coated with oil, it has a major leak somewhere. Maybe just a loose rocker-arm cover; maybe not. Check the transmission fluid and main oil supply. If the former emits a burnt odor, shy away from the car. Look at the battery; is there a build-up of corrosion? cables eaten away? battery hold-down clamp broken or missing?

Even if you don't know that much about a car yet, you can get an idea of how the car was maintained by such things as oil accumulations, condition of wires, etc.

The inside of the car can give you a tipoff as to the way it was taken care of. Worn or broken aremrests, knobs missing from their handles, worn carpeting, the manner in which the doors open and close are all signs of a car that has been used hard. Incidentally, if you're looking at a car that registers unusually low mileage for its age, the just-mentioned conditions are a tipoff that the car could have more miles on it than registered on the odometer.

If you're still interested in a certain car once you've given it a thorough inspection, the next obvious step is to drive it.

The engine shouldn't have to turn over much before it fires. And it should turn vigorously. If the engine sounds as though it's laboring to start, the battery and/or starter could be bad. Once the engine starts, the idiot lights (small red or orange lights on the instrument panel) for the alternator, and brakes, should go out immediately.

With the engine idling, put the transmission into gear. If it's automatic, a slight clunk should follow immediately as the gear is engaged. If the transmission hesitates a couple of seconds or longer, it could mean that it's about to go out. With standard transmission, put it into gear and let the clutch pedal out slowly, with the emergency brake on.

If the pedal comes almost all the way out, before the clutch engages, the clutch may be shot, or just need adjustment. But figure on the worse, just in case. Stand on the brake pedal to see if the pedal sinks to the floor. If it does, there's a leak somewhere in the brake system.

19

Turn the steering wheel from side to side to see if there is too much free motion or if it makes clunking sounds.

A road test will tell you a lot more about a car. Does it accelerate smoothly? If not, it may need a tune-up. How's the steering? Does the car want to crawl to one side of the road? If so, the front end is out of alignment. Accelerate briskly, then let up on the gas. Look into the rear-mirror to see if any blue clouds erupt from the tail pipe. If they do, you're driving an oil burner that needs at least a fuel pump.

If possible, drive the car over a bumpy road to see how the suspension and steering reacts. If either is bad, you'll know it by the way the car jumps around.

After you've inspected and driven the car, now comes a little serious thought. What did you find wrong with it? Make a mental or written checklist of everything you've found in doubtful or poor condition. Weigh the cost of their repair or replacement against the ''asking'' price of the car.

If you can do many of the repairs yourself, and if you can get the car at your price, you're money ahead.

But if major work is called for, and you still want the car, check with a garage for estimates. If the selling party is an individual, ask if it would be all right to have the car checked first by a garage or by a knowledgeable person. If the seller refuses to have the car checked over, he might be trying to cover up something.

If you're shopping for a particular model and brand car, ask mechanics who work on that particular model what faults to look for. In this way, you can look for specific problem areas that might normally escape your attention.

Furthermore, some of the chapters in this book can help you troubleshoot certain components that might be faulty. Go back over those chapters before you go shopping.

Hopefully, you'll find that dream car at a good price. So, start looking…and good luck!

Part II
PERFORMANCE GAS MILEAGE
AND
THE CHARTS

Chapter 5

HOW TO DOUBLE YOUR GAS MILEAGE

You'd like to double your gas mileage. Okay, it's possible, but first let's see what happens when the engine converts the gasoline to energy.

Engine design today makes it possible for about 35% of that energy to be converted into motion. Realistically, only about 12% of it is used to move the car. The engine uses some of the energy to keep itself running; other systems use some for their operation; power assisted devices use some, too. All together, it's not a very efficient system. Wherever you have heat in the car such as radiates from the engine, the radiator, the exhaust, the tires and the brakes—you have energy that's not being used to move the car, and therefore, is not contributing to your miles per gallon.

Ignition, valve timing and fuel metering (the carburetor's function), must be quite accurate for the engine to function efficiently. It doesn't take much of a maladjustment to stop it completely.

The amount of energy needed to move your car is determined by its rolling resistance, which is determined by the car's weight and frontal area. Speed does not effect the energy drain under 30 or 40 miles per hour. Over that speed, it gets progressively harder to push the frontal area through the air. Streamlining lowers the air resistance to a degree.

What can you do to raise your miles per gallon? If you want to consider a big gesture, think about getting a smaller, lighter-weight car. There is no way a large, heavy car can be as energy efficient as a small light one. At highway speeds, a large frontal area fighting wind resistance, calls for a lot of power (energy) which means a large engine. A large engine's weight means the related components must be heavier. Under 40 miles per hour, weight is the major factor in rolling resistance. And, the amount of energy necessary to move a given weight stays pretty much the same at any speed. You can't avoid using more energy in a heavy car even if you don't turn the key.

A great deal of energy is used to process a pound of steel or plastic, so even before you start it up, a two-thousand pound car is more energy efficient than a five-thousand pound car.

But, there are ways of sharpening the performance of any car. All of the tune up and maintenance adjustments in the owner's manual and Shop Manual for your car are stated with a lower and an upper limit. These two numbers are the tolerance limits, which means that an adjustment measurement that falls anywhere in between is okay. Usually though, the adjustment will be more efficient at some more accurate point within the limits. For example, the tire pressure. Say the owner's manual recommends 28 to 32 lbs. pressure (under different load conditions). You know that the tires will wear well and be safe with any amount of pressure in between. But since a hard tire has less drag than a soft one, we set the tires at 32 lbs. and it takes less energy to keep them rolling. Comfort is the reason for the lower limit. Give a little, get a little.

If we tune all of the adjustment more accurately to their most efficient points and be more diligent about keeping them tuned, we can have better performance, more consistent performance, and longer life.

Many products on the market claim that they will give you a significant improvement in gas mileage. Unfortunately, in most instances they just don't work. This is not to say that they don't have some value as part of a totally modified system or in getting the car to start easier.

There is one magical component in this system that can really increase your miles per gallon by ten, twenty or thirty percent. You. What you choose to do and how you do it. You can significantly improve your miles per gallon by rethinking your driving habits. Do you tap the gas pedal two or three times before you turn the key to start? Those taps use gas. Is that a habit you got into with a car years ago that needed those taps? Maybe your present car will start easier without them, or maybe one will do perfectly. Do you have a habit of letting the car warm for a couple of minutes before moving off? Modern cars with modern lubricants don't need that. Move the controls gently and tread lightly on the gas for the first few minutes and you can move immediately. Moving gently and treading lightly help tremendously even after the car is warmed up.

24

Slamming the gas down to get rolling to the next stop light, throws away a large quantity of gas, and slamming your foot on the brakes to stop, dissipates that energy (while simultaneously wearing away the brake linings).

A simple but not exaggerated example: Driving in town through a series of stop lights timed for 28 miles per hour, rushing from one light to the next in first and second gear, stopping for a moment and then rushing the same way to the next light, can use almost three times the amount of gas necessary to drive this same distance at a steady 28 miles per hour. And, you don't even get there any faster! Steadiness works on an expressway, too. Pick your speed and try to vary it as little as possible. By watching the traffic a little further ahead of you, as well as behind you, you will be able to manage passing and being passed without accelerating or braking. (Being more aware of other people on the road just happens to be safer, too.)

Try to be steady and smooth. You've heard that advice in regard to handling a blow-out or driving in the rain or snow or on glare ice. It helps on a warm, dry sunny day, too. It helps you to improve your miles per gallon because the engine is most efficient when it's running at a steady speed. An engine's performance is at it's worst when accelerating or de-accelerating. Any movement of your gas pedal is lowering that steady-state efficiency, and the larger the movement, the greater the effect. Smoothness counts.

Speed effects mileage. The speed at which you choose to drive can vary your miles per gallon dramatically because as you double your speed the energy necessary to overcome wind resistance increases on the square. At 60 miles per hour you burn four times as much gas as you do at 30 miles per hour. Keeping your speed under 60 miles per hour will give you a noticeable improvement in miles per gallon.

There are ways of getting better performance from your car. The degree of improvement is up to you.

What will help improve performance:
—Frequent and regular maintainance
—More accurate tuning
—Thoughtfulness about driving
—Careful consideration while driving
—Finesse behind the wheel

This is how the machines work and this is why they work the way they do. What do you want your car to do? How do you want it to do it? It's up to you.

Chapter 6

THE TROUBLE-SHOOTER CHARTS

HOW TO USE THEM

If you've gotten interested in the condition of your car and have begun a maintenance program, you may never need these CHARTS. However, if you discover a symptom, you can keep it from turning into a problem by referring to the CHARTS first. It's so much easier to do a small chore in the comfort of your garage with your tools handy, than it is trying to figure out what to do on the side of a deserted country road on a rainy night.

If you can't locate your symptom on one CHART, look further. As you're looking, you may recognize symptoms you didn't know were there.

Some of the descriptions are subjective. For example, in the NOISE TROUBLE-SHOOTER, what I may hear as "Chuff," someone else may hear as "Psst." "Clank" to me is a "hitting a flag pole with a broom handle" sound. "Clunk" is more like "a sledge hammer dropped on the floor in the next room." "Whir" is a faster, lighter-weight "Grind," which is a higher-pitched "Growl."

Even if you are coming to this activity with no experience at all, the TROUBLE-SHOOTER CHARTS should be able to help you. Read them carefully. Start with The Symptom, move to The Cause, then go on to The Remedy.

If you have doubts about your findings, ask a knowledgeable person to confirm them. Quite often your shop manual will give more detailed symptoms pertaining to your particular model car. And, if something does seem to be going awry, at least you can be more specific in describing what your problem is when the car refuses to act up for the mechanic.

27

But, most of the maintenance and TROUBLE-SHOOTING procedures are simple and need no special knowledge or tools. When you're more confident, you can try some of the more involved tasks and get the particular tools necessary. The right tools make a job so much easier and generally pay for themselves the first or second time you use them.

In the meantime, keep the CHARTS handy and enjoy yourself.

Bill Takas

WHEN YOUR CAR WON'T START TROUBLE-SHOOTER

SYMPTOM	REMEDY
Engine dead (Will not turn on)	First, check battery.
Battery weak or dead	Try lights. If dim, the battery is weak. Look for looseness and corrosion on battery cables. Clean and tighten. If fan belt is loose, tighten. Jumper cables or a push should start the car.
If battery is okay	Look for looseness and corrosion at the starter end of battery cable. Clean and tighten cable connections.
If clean and tight at starter	Touch metal across solenoid terminals (see glossary). If starter works, ignition switch faulty. If it clicks, starter may be jammed. (See below.) If nothing happens, solenoid faulty. A push may start the car.
Starter jammed	With ignition switched off, put in high gear and push car one or two feet. Starter should pop loose.
Engine seized (jammed up, frozen)	As above. But, if seized, car won't move. If seizure is due to overheating, let it cool. It may start after cooling. Check oil and water.
Ignition switch may be faulty	Check loose wires and seat belt interlock and shift lever. Sensors may be at fault. See Shop Manual.
	See Shop Manual also for possibility of faulty components in system peculiar to your model car.
Starter turns, but won't start	Slight dampness can short circuit old, dried wires. Also dust on bakelight (plastic insulating material) part of coil and distributor cap (inside and outside). Heavy wetness will short the points and also the spark plugs. If available, try spraying with water repellent silicone lubricant or carbon tetrachloride. Try wiping everything dry.

If all wires tight and dry..	Check spark plugs. If spark from end of plug wire jumps ⅜" or more, plugs are faulty. Check the choke. If plugs are not greasy, in an emergency, you can close the gap to about ½ normal on just one or two plugs and engine should start. It will run poorly, but at least it will run.
Weak spark, (if spark from end of plug wires jumps less than ⅜")	See emergency above. Points or condenser are at fault. The coil is rarely at fault unless other parts of the system have been acting up. See Shop Manual.
No spark	See above, plus check rotor, coil and distributor cap for cracks and burns.
If there's spark, gas in the tank and all fuel and vacuum lines are secure.........................	Take air cleaner off the carburetor. If it looks dry, turn the engine over a few turns with your hands sealing air intake. Your hand should get wet with gas.
If carburetor is wet with gas......................................	The engine is flooded if you have not been trying to start if for a while. The float valve is probably stuck open. Tap side of carburetor. See Shop Manual.
If carburetor is not wet with gas	Something is plugged or the fuel pump isn't working. First unscrew gas cap in case air vent is plugged. Also, see Shop Manual in case you have an anti-dieseling valve that may be defective.
If you've been cranking the starter a lot....................	Wait a minute, then hold gas pedal steady on the floor (don't pump). It should start.

NOISE TROUBLE-SHOOTER

SYMPTOM	CAUSE	REMEDY
Light shriek when revving engine.	Loose fan belt	Set correct tension and lube with rubber lube.
Ding or shriek when applying brakes.	Glazed or wrong type of lining.	Sandpaper. If shine remains, replace.
Loud chirp or heavy shriek when steering wheel turned sharply.	Low fluid level in power steering.	Top up. Look for leaks. Correct. Get air out of lines (bleed).
Grinding or squeal when holding clutch pedal down.	Clutch throw-out bearing worn.	Replace.
Growl or grinding from corner of car varying with car speed.	Loose and probably worn wheel bearing.	Grease and tighten or replace.
Deep whirring in trunk area varying with car speed.	Dry or worn gears in differential.	Check for leak. Correct. Fill up. If noise persists, don't worry unless it gets noticeably louder from day to day or if you are towing a trailer.
Grinding in dashboard	Dry or kinked speedometer cable.	Disconnect from back of speedometer and spray Graphite into cable. If kinked, straighten or replace.
Shriek when air conditioner turned on.	Drive belt slipping Compressor jammed	Tighten. Recharge with freon. See Shop Manual.
Growl or grinding when brakes applied.	Linings worn	Replace linings and check discs or drums for smoothness. Replace if ridged.
Heavy rattle under middle of car.	Loose or misaligned exhaust system.	Tighten or realign. Replace if broken.
Heavy rattle at corner of car.	Loose shock absorber or broken mount.	Tighten or replace.
Clanking under car varying with speed.	Worn universal joint	Rebuild or replace. See Shop Manual.

Clunk when turning .... steering wheel.	Worn joints in steering linkage.	Replace.
	Worn steering gear box.	Replace.
Clunking when crossing .... bumps.	Worn ball joints in .... suspension.	Replace. See Shop Manual.
Loud exhaust, but comes .... from front.	Exhaust manifold gasket bad.	Replace. See Shop Manual.
Tires squeal at low speeds	Front wheels out of .... alignment.	Have wheels realigned.
Irregular knock or ticking .... when revving motor.	Bad gasoline	Try a tankful of higher octane gasoline.
	Timing retarded..................	Reset timing.
Even light knock when .... revving motor.	Worn pistons or bearings.	Use heavier weight oil and tread lighter on gas pedal. If it gets louder in a short period of time or distance, STOP! It's all over.
Constant tick varying with ...... engine speed.	Valve noise from low.......... oil level. or,	Top up oil level.
	Worn tappet	Adjust valves.
No tick, or fast tick in............. turn signal.	Burnt fuse or bulb	Replace.
	Loose wire or ground........	See Electric Trouble-Shooter.
Ticking in one particular gear. varying with car speed.	Chipped tooth in that gear. Possible danger from piece jamming other gears.	Very complicated to replace. Car may be driven. Use only other gears. Try draining transmission oil to get broken piece out and refill. Otherwise rebuild.
Chuffing in motor...................	One or more cylinders ...... not working.	
Idle, not smooth	Bad spark plug..................	Replace.
	Spark plug wire shorting .... or loose.	Make sure wires are separated. If burnt spot on one, replace.
	Burnt valve........................	Check compression. Grind valves.
Chuffing with idle smooth	Bad manifold gasket	Replace.

Thumping from tires	Flat spot on tread...............	Replace.
	Some tires "settle" when parked.	Thump usually goes away within a mile or two.
Tick, but no horn when........... horn button pressed.	Dirt, rust or water .... obstructing horn.	Clean.
	Loose or broken wire .... from relay to horn.	Tighten or connect.
Creaking when car .... bounces.	Dry joints...........................	Lubricate thoroughly.
Creaking when opening .... doors.	Dry hinges.........................	Oil.
Static in radio from .... engine or heater, etc.	Loose antenna..................	Tighten.
	Bad condenser or .... noise suppressor.	Replace. See Shop Manual or radio man.
Backfiring	Leak in exhaust system ..... Anti-backfire valve in	Reseal.
	A.I.R. malfunctioning..........	See Shop Manual.
	Ignition timing off...............	Reset timing.
Galloping engine idle...................	Clogged carburetor or........ air intake.	Replace air filter.
	Malfunctioning choke.........	Free linkage.
	Incorrect idle adjustment....	Reset idle speed screw and/or idle mixture. (See Shop Manual)
Cough in carburetor .... when you step on gas.	Accelerator pump............... malfunction.	Adjust.

FUEL SYSTEM TROUBLE-SHOOTER

SYMPTOM	CAUSE	REMEDY
Cough in the carb when you step on gas.	Engine not warm: Thermostat not working	Replace thermostat.
	Engine warm: Accelerator pump malfunction.	Adjust according to Service Manual.
Idle speed too high	Choke or idle cam stuck	Tap throttle or move either choke or throttle linkage by hand.
	Loose or cracked vacuum tube on intake manifold.	Tighten or replace.
Engine warm, but stalls	Idle speed too low	Adjust idle speed screw on throttle linkage.
Weak acceleration	Timing retarded	Reset timing.
	Pedal or linkage blocked	Clear obstruction.
Low miles per gallon	Gasoline leak	Find leak and tighten line or replace seal.
	Carb wet	Leak in carb. See Shop Manual.
	Idle speed too high	Adjust idle speed screw on throttle linkage.
	Carrying heavy load or towing a trailer.	C'est la vie.
	Air conditioner in constant use.	Turn off when not necessary.
	Clogged air cleaner	Replace.
	Choke stuck	Free choke.
	Faulty points, plugs, coil condenser or timing.	See Ignition Trouble Shooter.
	Overheating	See Cooling System Trouble Shooter.
	Temperature not up to normal.	Faulty thermostat, replace.
	Tire pressures low.	Reinflate to normal.
	Vibration loosened idle mixture screw.	Reset.

Symptom	Cause	Remedy
Shutting off ignition does not stop engine.	Bad spark plugs, points and/or condenser.	Replace.
	Anti-Diesel device faulty,	Replace. (See Shop Manual.)
	Bad gasoline	Try a tank of higher octane.
Engine won't start	See WHEN YOUR CAR WON'T START CHART.	
	Check fuel gauge and tank.	If gauge okay, fill tank.
	Choke stuck closed	Move by hand, free up.
	No gas. Choke stuck open.	As above.
	Flooded choke open	Needle valve stuck. Tap on side of carb. See Shop Manual.
	Choke okay, but no gas	Check fuel pump for dirt in line.
(Cold weather)	Frozen line	Put dri-gas in tank and carb.
(Hot weather)	Vapor lock in line	Let cool.
Stalls frequently	Choke or float valve	See above.
	Idle speed too low	Reset.
	Water in Gas	Use dri-gas in tank.
	Dirt in Gas	Replace filter.
	Air vent in gas cap or tank clogged.	Replace cap or reopen.
Power down	Fuel pump weak	Replace.
	Filter clogged	Replace.
	Ignition faulty	See Ignition Trouble Shooter.
	Other	See Low miles per gallon above.
Rattling in engine when accelerating.	Bad gasoline	Fill with higher octane.
	Timing retarded	Reset timing.

35

BRAKES TROUBLE-SHOOTER

SYMPTOM	CAUSE	REMEDY
Excessive pedal travel (more than 3 inches).	Air in system	Bleed brakes. Top up fluid.
	Low on fluid	Top up fluid.
	Brakes worn	If car does not have automatic adjusters, adjust brakes as per instructions. If automatic adjuster may be sticking, tap backing plates lightly.
Pedal goes to the floor quickly.	No fluid	Indicates bad hydraulic leak, broken line or cylinder. Find and replace.
Pedal goes to the floor slowly.	Bad seals in a cylinder	Best to rebuild or replace all cylinders.
Pedal feels spongy	Air or water in hydraulic lines.	Bleed brakes as per manual instructions.
Pedal occillates.	Drum out of round wheel bearing loose.	Take to machine shop to grind. If grinding noise while spinning, replace bearing.
Grinding or rumbling when brakes applied.	Worn linings	Replace.
Too much pressure needed on pedal.	Glazed linings	Sandpaper. If shine won't come out easily, replace.
	Power brake unit not working.	See Shop Manual.
Emergency brake won't hold.	Cable stretched	Adjust or replace as per Shop Manual
	Rear brakes worn	Adjust or replace as per Shop Manual
Loud squealing on new brakes.	Glazed lining	Sandpaper. If noise comes back, lining may be too soft. Replace.
	No glaze. Lining too hard for application.	Replace.
Brakes pull to one side.	Uneven tire pressure	Fill tires.
	Dirt or rust on discs or drums.	Drive very slowly holding brake on for about 50 yards.
	Bad wheel alignment	Have wheels realigned.

36

IGNITION TROUBLE-SHOOTER

SYMPTOM	CAUSE	REMEDY
Engine won't turn over	Battery dead	Charge.
	Cables loose and corroded.	Clean and tighten.
	Starter jammed	See WHEN YOUR CAR WON'T START Chart.
	Engine seized	If hot let cool. If not see WHEN YOUR CAR WON'T START Chart.
	Loose wires at starter	Clean and tighten.
	Solenoid or starter faulty	Replace.
	Ignition switch faulty	Replace.
Engine turns but won't start	Wet short	Dry everything and see WHEN YOUR CAR WON'T START Chart.
	Faulty spark plugs	Replace.
	Faulty ballast resistor	Replace.
	Loose wires at coil	Tighten.
	Faulty points, condenser. or coil.	Replace.
	Timing off	Reset timing.
Engine starts, but stalls immediately.	Faulty ballast resistor	Replace.
Engine runs, but stalls frequently.	Loose or shorting wires	Tighten.
	Weak spark	Check plugs, points, condenser and coil. Replace if necessary.
	Fuel System faulty	See FUEL SYSTEM TROUBLE-SHOOTER.
Engine idles lumpy	One or more bad spark plugs.	Disconnect plug wires one at a time. Whichever ones *do not* cause engine idle to drop are faulty.
	Too rich mixture	See FUEL SYSTEM TROUBLE-SHOOTER.

37

BODY ELECTRIC SYSTEM TROUBLE-SHOOTER

SYMPTOM	CAUSE	REMEDY
Lights do not turn on	Burnt out blub	Replace.
	Burnt out fuse	Replace.
	Dead battery	Recharge and correct.
	Loose connection in circuit .	Tighten.
	Corroded connection	Clean and tighten.
	Corroded switch	Replace.
Lights dim	Faulty bulbs	Replace.
	Loose or dirty connection.... in circuit.	Clean and tighten (check ground).
	Faulty voltage regulator	See Shop Manual.
Stop lights don't work	Check above, plus switch .. on brake master cylinder.	As above or replace switch.
Turn signals don't work	Burnt blub or fuse	Replace.
	Faulty flasher unit	Replace.
Headlight dimmer doesn't work.	Burnt out bulb or fuses	Replace.
	Faulty solenoid or switch ...	Replace.
	Loose or corroded connection.	Clean and tighten.
Windshield wiper repeatedly burns fuses.	Self-parking mechanism .... faulty.	See Shop Manual to correct.
Seat belt interlock or key buzzer not working.	Bad connection	See Shop Manual for junction sites.
No lights, but bulbs and fuses okay.	Corrosion in socket	Scrape socket so shiny metal makes contact.
	Socket ground bad	Tighten socket mount screws.
Bulb good, but fuse blows	Short circuit	Look for frayed wire, following wiring diagram in Shop Manual.
Fuse good, but bulb blows	Wrong or faulty bulb	Replace.
Battery not old, but runs down easily.	Loose fan belt	Tighten.
	Loose or corroded cables ..	Tighten and clean.
	Voltage regulator bad	Test as per Shop Manual and, if bad, replace.
	Alternator bad	Test as per Shop Manual and, if bad, replace.
	Check water level	Adjust water level.

COOLING SYSTEM TROUBLE-SHOOTER

SYMPTOM	CAUSE	REMEDY
Fluid loss	Leak	Look for wet or rust-stained area in hose. Replace. If hole in radiator, see Shop Manual.
	Loose belt	Tighten.
	Pressure leak	Replace radiator cap.
	Overheating	See constant over heat
Constant Overheating	Clogged radiator	Clear of bugs, mud. Flush radiator
	Clogged heater	Flush heater.
	Hose getting soft	Squeeze. If not uniformly firm, replace.
	Thermostat not working	Replace thermostat.
(With air conditioner)	Radiator not matched to air conditioner.	Replace radiator.
	Timing retarded	Reset timing.
Heater not working	Loose or broken dash control cable	Tighten or replace.
	Temperature control valve defective	May be jammed. Try to move with pliers or replace.
	Heater clogged	Flush heater.
Heater blower not working	Fuse burnt out	Replace.
	Obstruction in blower	With switch and ignition OFF, try to move blower by hand. If free, check wires for broken or chafed insulation. Reconnect or tape.
	Blower motor burnt out. Usually jammed	Replace.
Fresh air part of heater not working	Dash control cable loose or broken	Tighten or replace.
	Fresh air hose from behind grille loose or broken.	Reclamp or replace.
Defroster not working	Debris obstructing pipe from blower	Clear out.
	Pipe from blower loose or broken	Reconnect or tape or replace.

39

DRIVE TRAIN SUSPENSION AND STEERING TROUBLE-SHOOTER

SYMPTOM	CAUSE	REMEDY
Heavy steering	Tire pressure low	Inflate to correct pressure.
	Wheel alignment bad	Realign wheels.
	Steering power unit bad	If fluid level okay, replace
	Steering gear box adjustment.	Loosen adjuster or replace box
Loose steering	Wheel bearings worn	Replace.
	Linkage worn	Replace joints.
	Worn shocks	Replace.
	Steering gear box worn	Replace.
Pulling to one side	Tire pressure uneven	Inflate to correct pressure.
	Wheel alignment bad	Realign wheels.
	Brakes worn	Replace linings.
	Weak or broken springs	See Shop Manual to replace.
Excessive tire wear	Tire pressure low	Inflate to correct pressure.
	Wheel alignment	Realign wheels.
	Worn suspension	Replace ball joints.
	Wheel balance bad	Rebalance wheels.
Shimmy	Wheel balance bad	Rebalance wheels.
	Wheel alignment	Realign wheels.
	Too much free play	Adjust steering free play.
Clutch slip	Worn	Adjust or replace.
Clutch grab	Disc glazed	Replace.
	Disc cracked	Replace.
	Loose engine mount	Replace engine mount.
Noise in clutch	Throw out worn bearing	Replace.
Gears grind on shifts	Clutch does not disengage.	Adjust clutch.
	Warped disc	Replace.
	Release linkage stuck	Lubricate.

OTHER—SEE NOISE TROUBLE SHOOTER

40

DAILY—WEEKLY—MONTHLY—SEASONAL MAINTENANCE CHECKLIST

DAILY	WEEKLY	MONTHLY
Check Gas Gauge	Check Tire Pressure	Check Radiator Level
Check Tires	Check Lights	Check Battery Level
Check Seat Belts	Check Wipers	Check Radiator Hoses
Check Seat Adjustment	Check for leaks—oil,	Check Fan Belt
Pump Brakes BEFORE Moving	transmission, brakes,	Check Automatic Transmission
	radiator hoses	Fluid
		Check Brake Fluid
		Check Power Steering Fluid
		Check for Loose Wires
		Check Windshield Fluid

SEASONAL

Spring—Apply Rubber Preservative

Fall—Apply Rubber Preservative
    Apply Graphite to Speedometer Cable and Door Locks

Winter—Check U-Joints
    Check Exhaust System

Follow Service Shop Manual or Owner's Manual specs for mileage-related checks, lube, oil change, and filters.

Part III
PERFORMANCE MAINTENANCE AND DRIVING

Chapter 7

THE TOOLS YOU'LL NEED

Before you can do much work on your car, you're going to need certain basic tools. We'll look first at the tools the weekend mechanic usually needs most. Items like wrenches, screwdrivers, and pliers are the basic necessities for routine maintenance, but the handiest item of all will be a shop service manual for your particular make and model car. Because each model car is different in engine detail and layout of various components, you should have a comprehensive service manual to use in conjunction with this book. The manual will give you all the detailed information and instructions about how to proceed, and is usually well photographed. If you get into tune-ups and more involved tasks, the manual is invaluable because most owner's manuals don't include specific data. A shop service manual can usually be gotten through the Parts Department of your local car dealer.

The quality of tools should be given consideration. For infrequent maintenance, you don't need to invest a fortune in "professional" tools, but a decent quality set will last a lifetime and work just as well on a mower, bicycle, trailer, boat or sewing machine. The idea is to stay away from .89¢ dime-store tools without spending a lot of money for items you won't use as often as a professional mechanic would. Sears Roebuck tools are a good quality at a fair price and are easily obtainable.

Another consideration should be the standard of measurement you will be working with. American cars did use the S.A.E. standard, but are now phasing into the Metric system which the rest of the world utilizes. Metric nuts and bolts, in the most commonly used sizes, seem to coincide with S.A.E. sizes and, since U.S. industry is shifting to that standard, you probably will do well to get Metric-sized tools. English cars (excepting Ford) use a Whitworth standard of measure which is unfortunate as these sizes do not seem to match up with any of the others.

WRENCHES

There are three basic wrench types: open end, box end, and socket. Open end wrenches are slow, have a tendency to slip off tight nuts and when they do, they round off the edges of the nut making it more difficult to remove. The one advantage to the open wrenches is that they can slide on from the side (on a fuel line for example, where it's impossible to use a box, which must fit over the top).

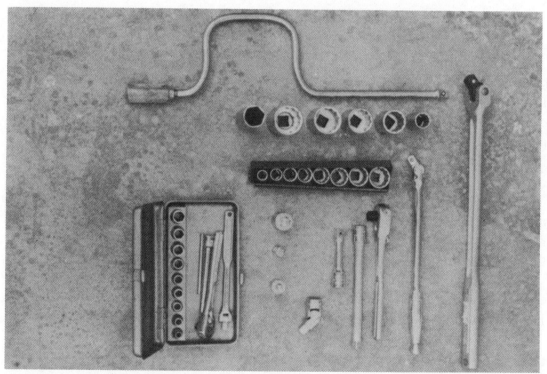

After you've added the basic wrenches to your tool box, you might want to include sockets sets and their accessories. Shown are three different-size drive socket sets: a ¼-drive set; a ⅜-drive set; and some ½-drive sockets, which are used for heavier nuts and bolts. The crank-shaped speed handle can come in handy at times, but it's not nearly as necessary as the ratchet, extensions, and breaker bars. Other useful items are the adapters that allow different size sockets to be used with other-size ratchets and breaker bar drives. A universal joint is helpful getting into tight places with sockets.

A 3/8 inch drive socket wrench set is very desirable and useful. All but the cheapist sets include a ratchet handle and extensions which make it a real time saver in simple speed and ability to reach into tight places.

Box-end wrenches are most useful in places where you cannot use a socket. In different places you will find that only one of these types will work because of the clearance problem. Therefore, it is best you have a set of each. A small saving can be made by getting a set with one boxed and the other open.

Although an adjustable wrench has a place in your toolbox, use it only when you don't have a suitably sized wrench. An adjustable wrench doesn't provide as precise a fit as does a specific-size wrench.

One special tool that you should give serious thought to investing in is a torque wrench. Tightening certain bolts and nuts on an engine requires critical tightening limits. The purpose of the torque wrench is to make sure that a nut or bolt is tightened precisely to a certain poundage. Some do-it-yourself sticklers torque everything from sparkplugs to wheel lug nuts. A versatile torque wrench should have at least a 150-pound capacity.

Allen wrenches, those hexagonal-shaped, L-formed tools will be needed at times. Keep a complete set in your toolbox.

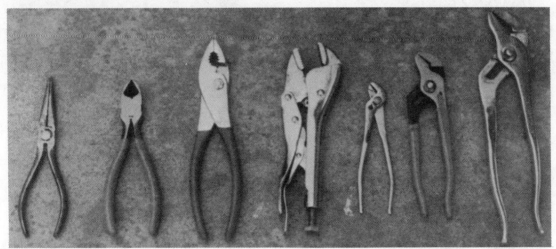

Other tool "musts" for the do-it-yourselfer are a selection of pliers. From left: needlenose pliers are needed for getting into very small areas; next to them are wire cutters, regular pliers, vise grips, ignition pliers, and interlocking pliers.

SCREWDRIVERS

In addition to a variety of wrenches, you'll also need an assortment of slotted-head and Phillips-head screwdrivers. Because of the countless and varying-sized screws on a car, you should have at least three different sized screwdrivers of each type.

PLIERS

Pliers are other mainstays of the do-it-yourselfer.

In addition to a pair of conventional pliers, you should have at least one pair of needlenose pliers for those hard-to-get-at places. Channel lock pliers are definitely an asset as the range of jaw travel they have makes them invaluable for a variety of uses.

Vise grips or locking pliers are another form of skin saver when it comes to gripping something with a lot of force.

HAMMERS

You'll need a ball peen hammer from time to time to free certain stubborn items. It would be wise to have two ball peen hammers: a small one for light pounding, and a heavy one for rough duty. A rubber or plastic mallet will come in handy for certain items that need a little persuasion without getting broken or marked up.

JACKS

If you plan on getting into much under-the-car work, get a hydraulic jack, jack stands or drive-up ramps. These items pay for themselves in convenience when it comes to changing oil, or doing lube or brake adjustments.

Don't be tempted to crawl under a car held up by only a bumper jack. If you don't have jack stands, use cement blocks underneath the axles to support the car.

Sad to say, more than one do-it-yourselfer has been crushed by his car when the bumper jack slipped. Safety first.

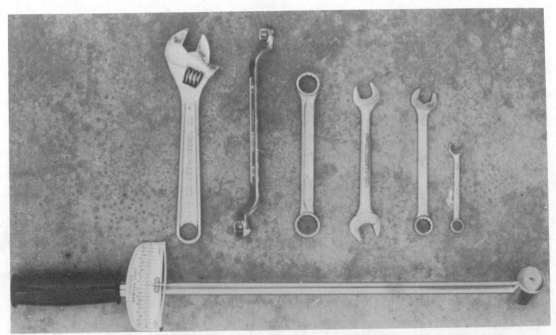

For general maintenance, you'll need an assortment of wrenches. Shown at the bottom is a torque wrench, so useful for obtaining proper tightening on everything from spark plugs to wheel lug nuts. From left to right: adjustable wrench; offset box-end wrench; box-end design; open-end type; combination box and open-end wrench; and a small ignition wrench for working in confined areas like the distributor.

You'll need a variety of screwdrivers for the myriad screws you'll find on a car. Basically, there are two designs of screw heads: Phillips head and the slotted heads. However, there are many different sizes of them. From left, ratcheting screwdriver with both Phillips head and slotted-head bits; and an assortment of Phillips and slotted-head screwdrivers. On the extreme right is a slotted head design that has a spring attachment for holding a screw in place when working in confined spaces.

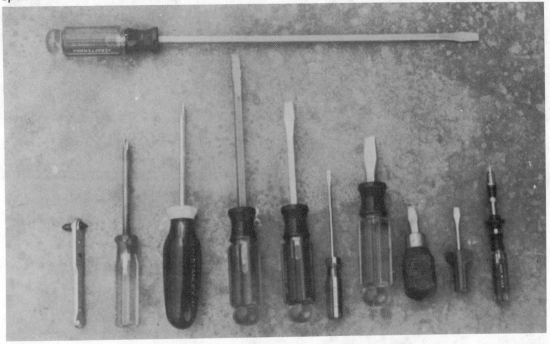

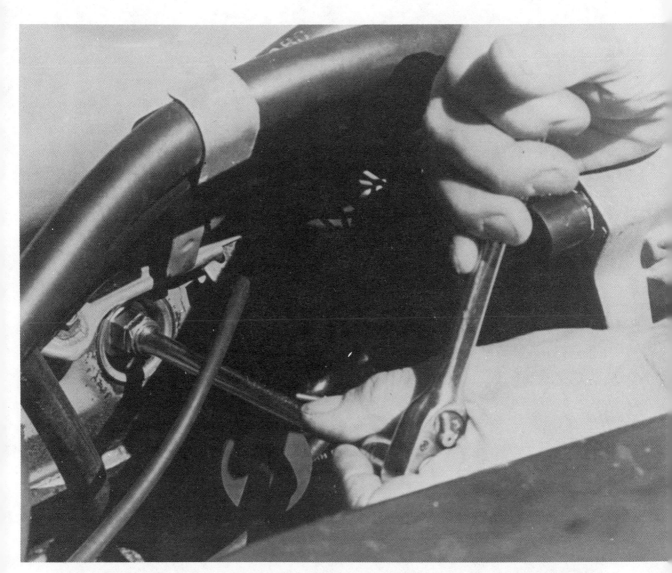

Even a simple job as removing spark plugs requires special tools to make the job easier. Here a ratchet wrench, extension, and special spark plug socket are used. Not all engines have this much room to work in, though.

OTHER NEEDED TOOLS

Spark plug gap-measuring gauges will certainly be necessary tools for conducting tune-ups.

Even the battery has its own special kinds of tools for keeping it up to par. For instance, there's a wire-brush post cleaner for removing current-impeding corrosion from the terminals. Corrosion can prevent adequate current from flowing to the rest of the electrical system. An alternative to the post-cleaner brush is a stiff-bristled wire brush.

Keep a tire air gauge in the glove compartment, and use it frequently. Low tire pressure cuts down the gas mileage and increases tire wear. Uneven tire pressures can make the braking uneven, the steering unstable, and the stability of the whole car downright dangerous!

The more involved you become with car maintenance, the more tools and accessories you'll find a need for. But, if you're just starting out, worry only about the basic tools and equipment as covered in this chapter. Then, if your interest and pocketbook so dictate, add to your basics.

But, one step at a time.

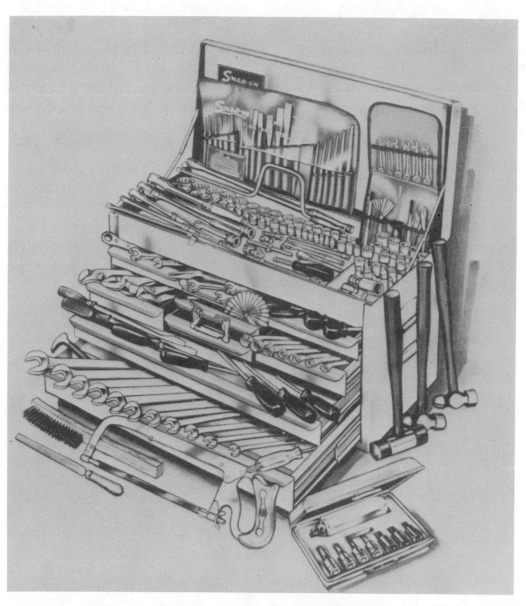

You won't need this complete of a toolset to perform minor maintenance on your car, but if you ever become serious about doing most of your own work, a fine toolset like this is needed.

Chapter 8

YOUR TIRES

Regardless of what your car's performance capability is, it's all to no avail if there is not a good set of tires to transfer that performance to the ground.

Just think: they're your only link with the road...four small patches of rubber! You can't afford to take chances with them!

But, that's just what a lot of motorists do—trust their fate to any old set of tires. Hopefully, you're not one of them. This chapter is intended to make you even more "tire conscious" by showing you some things about tires that you possibly did not know before.

Even if you are well versed on those rubber "skins", you might find yourself ignoring them more than you should. Before you start wondering when the last time was that you looked them over, read on.

TIRE TERMINOLOGY

When you go shopping for tires, you should have some idea of tire terminology. One term often mentioned in tire talk is ply. It is a layer of nylon or polyester that runs from bead to bead. The bead is the wire-reinforcement inner circumference of the tire that holds it on the wheel. Since tires usually have two or more plies in their construction, they are arranged at angles to each other to give the tire its rigidity and

TYPES OF TIRE CONSTRUCTION

Bias-Ply

Belted-Bias

Radial

NOTE: Each tire has an air-tight inner-liner under the body plies. The belted-bias and the radial tires also have under-tread belts, which are shown with a gray tone.

RESULTS OF IMPROPER CARE

Suspension Neglect

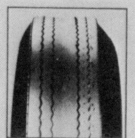
Over-Inflation

Under-Inflation

Extreme Cornering

The Firestone Tire & Rubber Company

performance characteristics.

The number of plies in a tire has decreased from six of years ago to as low as two plies in a modern tire. Improvement in both design and construction of tires over the years has made them much better than their forerunners.

Heat is the enemy of a tire, and the more plies there are to flex against each other and generate friction, the more heat the tire will generate. Excessive heat shortens a tire's life.

Belt is another term you'll often hear in a discussion of tires. It's a layer, or "belt", of material, like fiberglass or steel cord that runs around the circumference of a tire instead of from bead to bead. The primary purpose of the belts is to keep the tread in better contact with the road.

There are three basic types of tires employed on cars today: bias ply, bias-belted and radial.

Usually of two-ply construction, the bias ply is the least expensive tire to buy. Recommended for moderate driving conditions only, the bias-belted, on the other hand, will allow a higher degree of performance under harder driving conditions than will the bias ply. In addition to its plies placed at angles to one another, the bias-belted type has two belts of steel or fiberglass which tend to hold the tread more firmly on the road.

The radial tire has plies that run straight across from bead to bead. Like the bias-belted design, the radial's plies are reinforced by circumferential belts. This tire provides superior roadholding and performance to the other two types of tire.

A significant advantage of a radial tire is that there's less friction between its plies and lower rolling resistance. Gas mileage and tire life both benefit from this reduced friction. For high-speed, harsh-service conditions, radial tires are the way to go. They cost more, but they can outlast conventional tires three to one. Good radials will usually be guaranteed up to 40,000 miles.

But because they are superior to other tires, radials must never be mixed with bias ply or bias-belted types, or the car's handling will suffer.

Mixing bias ply with bias-belted tires isn't as severe as mixing either of them with radials, but it still isn't advisable.

If you must have both bias ply tires and belted-bias tires on the same car, put the belted-bias on the back. Don't ever put bias ply on one side and bias-belted on the other side. Keep the tire size consistent at least on each end of the car. Having an odd-sized tire will affect handling.

55

SIZE

Picking the right-sized tires for your car requires some thought, too. Modern tire sizes are identified by a combination of letters and numbers. For example, a popular size today is an F78 × 14. The F denotes the wheel's rim width which would be 7.75 inches. The number 78 designates the height of the tire (measured from the bottom of the tread to the bead) and is 78% of the tire's width (measured from sidewall to sidewall). A 70 series tire would have a height of 70% of its width.

If the letter R is placed after the letter, it identifies the tire as a radial.

TIRE MAINTENANCE

The most important phase of tire maintenance is to make sure they're inflated properly. Here again is something most auto owners tend to neglect.

A tire gauge is one of the most important and least expensive tools you should have. Make it a habit to check tire pressures on a regular basis.

56

But, did you know that if you keep those "donuts" inflated properly you can lengthen their service life by as much as 30%? That means checking them once a week, at least. And if you drive considerable distances each week, that means you need to check them at least twice weekly.

Under-inflation is the big problem because even good tires will lose air to a certain extent. Furthermore, during cold weather, every 10 degree drop in temperature will lower a tire's pressure by one pound. Under-inflation can reduce a tire's life by as much as 60%, because a soft tire flexes and runs hotter. Besides the excess heat generated, the outside areas of the tread wear faster, too.

In addition, soft tires make the steering harder. They also become less responsive to your steering movement.

Over-inflation, if it's not pronounced, isn't as bad as under-inflation, but it'll make the tires more vulnerable to damage from impact with hard or sharp objects. Over-inflation also makes the center portion of the tread wear faster than the other areas.

It's important that the front tires match each other and that the back tires match each other. Otherwise the steering will suffer.

To keep after tires, avail yourself of a good tire-pressure guage. Don't rely on the ones at service stations, as many of them are grossly inaccurate.

Check the tires only when they're cold.

Warm tires will show an increase of anywhere from 3-6 pounds higher than when they are cold. You'll find the maximum inflation pressure on the sidewall. It won't hurt to go over the figure recommended by the owner's manual by a couple of pounds or so, but don't exceed the maximum-allowable pressure. Long-distance driving with heavy loads may require that you carry 2 or 3 pounds more pressure, as long as it's not over that maximum-allowable figure.

Wheel and tire balancing help the tires perform better and last longer. You might not think that a slightly out of balance tire would make that much difference. But a one-ounce imbalance will grow in force until, at 60 miles per hour, that one ounce is tugging on the tire with a 12-pound force.

An out-of-balance wheel or tire will make itself felt by sending a vibration through the car.

Sometimes a wheel can't be balanced because the tire itself is out of round.

When it comes to tire rotation, you can get into all kinds of arguments. Most owners' manuals still recommend it every 5000 miles to equalize tire wear and make

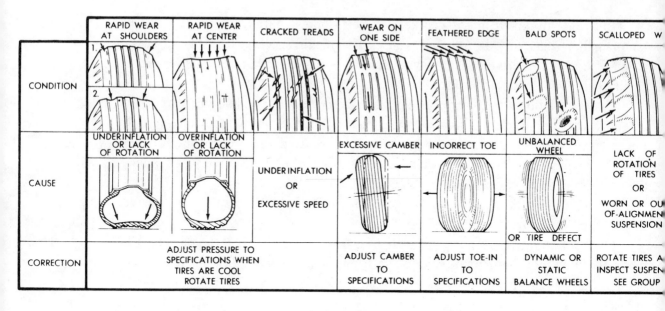

	RAPID WEAR AT SHOULDERS	RAPID WEAR AT CENTER	CRACKED TREADS	WEAR ON ONE SIDE	FEATHERED EDGE	BALD SPOTS	SCALLOPED W
CONDITION	1. 2.						
CAUSE	UNDER INFLATION OR LACK OF ROTATION	OVER INFLATION OR LACK OF ROTATION	UNDER INFLATION OR EXCESSIVE SPEED	EXCESSIVE CAMBER	INCORRECT TOE	UNBALANCED WHEEL OR TIRE DEFECT	LACK OF ROTATION OF TIRES OR WORN OR OU OF-ALIGNMEN SUSPENSION
CORRECTION	ADJUST PRESSURE TO SPECIFICATIONS WHEN TIRES ARE COOL ROTATE TIRES			ADJUST CAMBER TO SPECIFICATIONS	ADJUST TOE-IN TO SPECIFICATIONS	DYNAMIC OR STATIC BALANCE WHEELS	ROTATE TIRES A INSPECT SUSPEN SEE GROUP

Tire rotation.

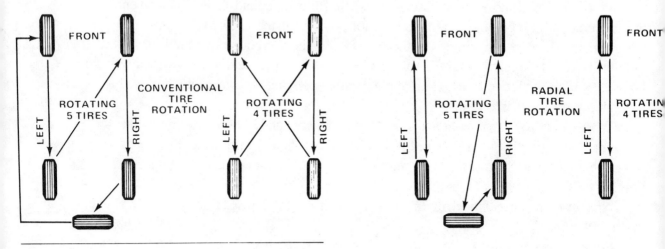

CONVENTIONAL TIRE ROTATION

ROTATING 5 TIRES

ROTATING 4 TIRES

RADIAL TIRE ROTATION

ROTATING 5 TIRES

ROTATIN 4 TIRES

them last longer. But some tire-knowledgeable types say that where the tires are changed from side to side, it can shorten a tire's life when its direction of rotation is reversed.

Wheel alignment is still something else that has a lot to do with the way the front tires wear. And in the chapter on steering and suspension, you'll see how the suspension components are altered to align the wheels.

Once you learn how to interpret wear patterns on your tires, you'll come to know just what is making a tire wear irregularly. For example, as already mentioned, over-inflation will make the center portion of the tread wear more quickly; under-inflation causes the outer tread areas to wear faster. If only one side of a tire wears faster than the other side it means that the wheel is angled incorrectly vertically.

If each tread rib has a slanted or "feathered" edge, it means that the wheels are toed in too much, or toed out too much. By toe-in, I mean that the front parts of the tires point inwardly, while toe-out denotes the exact opposite: the front areas of the tires point out to the sides.

Flat spots at different points on a tire indicate that the wheel or tire is out of balance. A scalloped pattern around the tire would suggest front-wheel misalignment or faulty suspension. Sometimes braking hard from high speed will produce flat spots on a tire. Hard cornering accelerates tire wear by grinding away the outer edges of the tires.

One of the quickest ways to hasten tire wear is to drive at high speeds. At 80 miles per hour, tires will wear five times faster than they will at 50-55. And it's always a good idea to keep the speed within the 50-60 mile an hour range for the first 500 miles to give new tires a chance to break in.

Modern tires have tread-wear bars in the tread that appear after the tire has worn enough tread away to warrant replacement. Whenever a tire has worn down to its last 1/16-inch of tread, replace the tire.

What about recapped tires? Are they safe?

Recaps are okay if the tires being recapped are in good condition and aren't going to be driven over 40 MPH anyway. If you use recapped tires for long-distance or high-speed driving, you're putting your life (and the lives of others) in jeopardy.

Tubeless tires are better than the old tube-type because they generate less heat.

Although blow-outs seem to be something of the past, tubeless tires can still go flat. The customary repair is to fix the hole with a plug from the outside, but the tire should be removed from the wheel and checked over carefully for a nail, piece of wire or other foreign object that might have worked its way inside. If that object isn't removed, it'll bounce around inside the tire and weaken it internally.

And don't forget to keep those tires properly inflated. Treat them as you would a friend. They need you, and you most certainly need them.

Chapter 9

YOUR BRAKES

Now that you have an idea of how to choose and maintain tires, what about the components that work directly with them? That's right, the brakes.

As important as tires are, they're not much good unless they have an effective braking system to bring them to a halt. Brakes are among the taken-for-granted components of a car. Tires you can see, but brakes...well, as long as they stop the car, why worry about them. It's when they don't stop the car well that we worry.

But because you're the type of driver who is concerned about getting the best out of his or her car, you don't want to wait until the brakes go bad before you pay attention to them.

HOW THE BRAKES WORK

There are two basic types of brakes on modern cars: the drum type and the disc. Both systems are hydraulically operated. When the brake pedal is depressed, it causes fluid in the master cylinder to be forced into slave cylinders which, in drum brakes, push curved shoes outward against the inner surfaces of the drums. Frictional contact is provided by high-temperature resistant pads on the shoes. The disc brake setup employs a steel disc with a caliper that has a slave cylinder and lined pad on either side of it, which squeezes the disc with tremendous pressure.

61

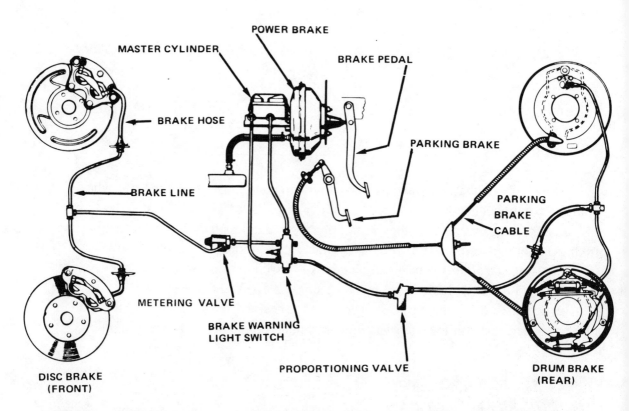

POWER BRAKE

MASTER CYLINDER

BRAKE PEDAL

BRAKE HOSE

PARKING BRAKE

BRAKE LINE

PARKING
BRAKE
CABLE

METERING VALVE

BRAKE WARNING
LIGHT SWITCH

PROPORTIONING VALVE

DISC BRAKE
(FRONT)

DRUM BRAKE
(REAR)

The accompanying illustration shows the various parts of a modern duo-design braking system, featuring disc brakes up front and conventional drum brakes in the rear.

Note the component called a metering valve: it restricts maximum hydraulic pressure to the front brakes, until the rear brake linings have a chance to "catch up" and make contact with their drums. The metering valve allows all four brakes to make contact at the same time. Without this device, the disc brakes would start braking first, before the rear brakes had a chance to come into play.

The parking brake is a mechanical system in which the rear-brake linings are pulled against the drums by means of a foot pedal or hand lever to hold the car when it's stationary.

A major part of maintaining both drum and disc brakes involves that of replacing the linings and the pads when a certain amount of their frictional material is worn away from use.

We'll look at both systems to see what basic maintenance you can undertake to keep them functioning.

One of the first steps you should undertake is to check the fluid level in the master cylinder. It should be almost to the top. Late model cars have a dual system. Some have two reservoirs. Some have one. One goes to the rear brakes and the other to the front brakes.

When topping up the master cylinder(s), use only a D.O.T. grade fluid. Why? Brake fluid is subjected to tremendous heat and pressure. A low-grade (non-D.O.T.) fluid might boil and that makes for instant no-brakes.

Of course, the brakes are only part of the overall picture of "doubling the performance of your car." But they're a vital part. And if there's one system that you should care about, it should be the brakes. Let this chapter serve as a stimulus for furthering your search for more knowledge and skill concerning better braking. Enough said.

Photograph of a rear drum brake.
A-Wheel cylinder; B-Backing plate; C-Brake shoe; D-Hold-down spring for brake shoe; E-Adjuster spring; F-Starwheel adjuster; G-Return springs; H-Lining; I-Pivot pin; J-Parking brake cable and housing; K-Parking-brake lever; L-Parking-brake strut.

On power brakes, check the vacuum line for secure attachment. Make sure there are no leaks anywhere, or braking effectiveness will be reduced.

Checking the brake fluid supply in the master cylinder is a simple procedure. Release the spring clip with a screwdriver and lift off the top. The fluid level should be almost near the top (arrow).

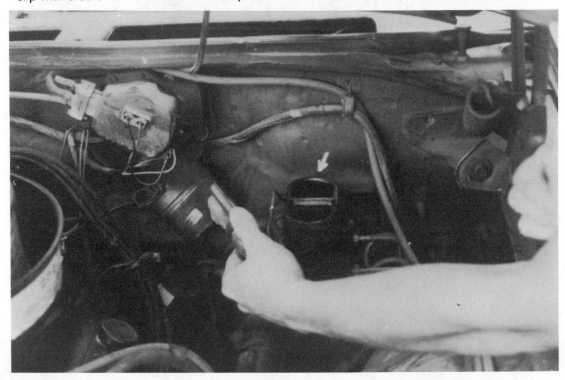

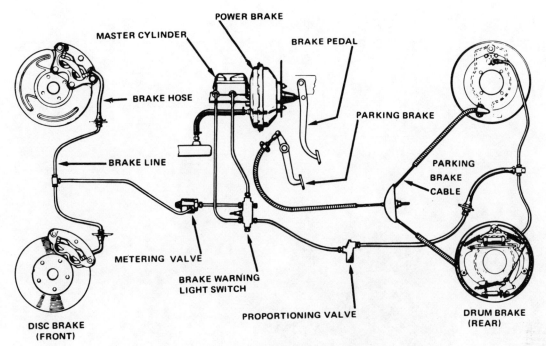

POWER BRAKE

MASTER CYLINDER

BRAKE PEDAL

BRAKE HOSE

PARKING BRAKE

BRAKE LINE

PARKING BRAKE CABLE

METERING VALVE

BRAKE WARNING LIGHT SWITCH

PROPORTIONING VALVE

DISC BRAKE (FRONT)

DRUM BRAKE (REAR)

Typical Modern Brake System.

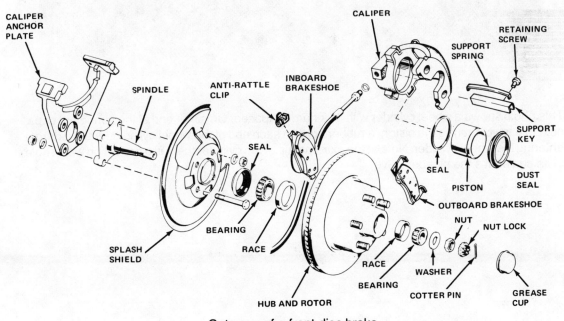

CALIPER ANCHOR PLATE

CALIPER

SUPPORT SPRING

RETAINING SCREW

SPINDLE

ANTI-RATTLE CLIP

INBOARD BRAKESHOE

SUPPORT KEY

SEAL

SEAL

PISTON

DUST SEAL

BEARING

OUTBOARD BRAKESHOE

SPLASH SHIELD

RACE

RACE

NUT

NUT LOCK

BEARING

WASHER

COTTER PIN

GREASE CUP

HUB AND ROTOR

Cutaway of a front disc brake.

This photo shows a wheel cylinder with its innards exposed. On either end of the spring are cups; next to each of them is the piston; a rubber boot on each end of the wheel cylinder keeps dirt from entering the wheel cylinder. Note at the extreme top of the cylinder there is a projection with a hole in its center: it's the bleeder valve.

Chapter 10

YOUR FUEL SYSTEM

Now, if you have your tools handy and are eager to get started, let's go on to the fuel system.

So, pop open the hood and take a peek inside the engine compartment. If you have a late-model car loaded with all kinds of options like air conditioning, power steering, and all those emissions controls, don't become alarmed at all that "plumbing." We're concerned only with the *basics* of making your car run better and saving money.

You don't need a degree in automotive engineering or a master mechanic's rating to do that. With that thought in mind, let's go under the hood and unravel some of the mysteries of the fuel system.

THE AIR FILTER

Because the air filter is the most accessible part of the fuel system, we'll start with it. Generally, you'll find it located in the central part of the engine compartment; it's a "pan-shaped" component that sits on top of the carburetor.

To get at the element, you'll have to remove the top of the filter housing by undoing a wing nut or two. With the top off, the filter element can be lifted out. Most cars use the disposable elements, which consist of a pleated-paper filtering material. If

67

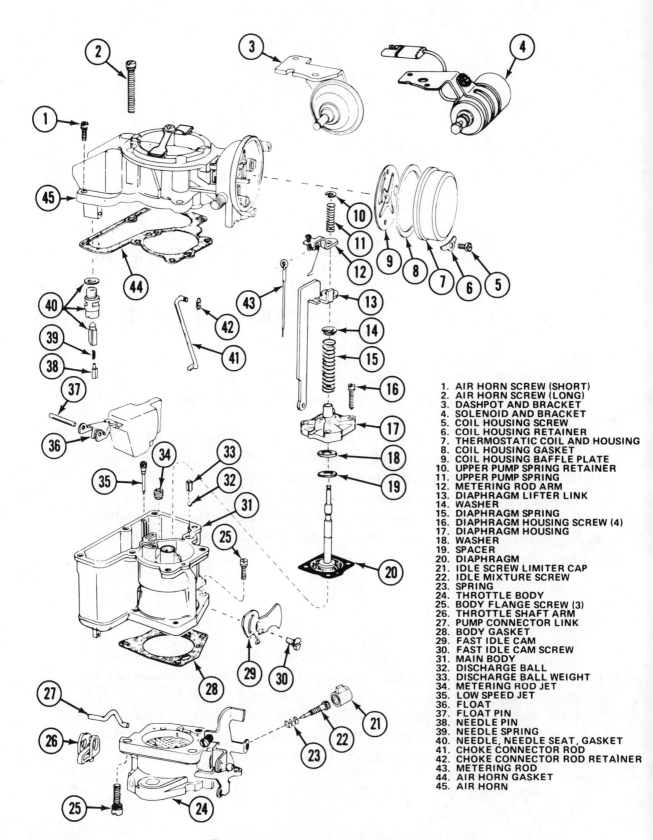

1. AIR HORN SCREW (SHORT)
2. AIR HORN SCREW (LONG)
3. DASHPOT AND BRACKET
4. SOLENOID AND BRACKET
5. COIL HOUSING SCREW
6. COIL HOUSING RETAINER
7. THERMOSTATIC COIL AND HOUSING
8. COIL HOUSING GASKET
9. COIL HOUSING BAFFLE PLATE
10. UPPER PUMP SPRING RETAINER
11. UPPER PUMP SPRING
12. METERING ROD ARM
13. DIAPHRAGM LIFTER LINK
14. WASHER
15. DIAPHRAGM SPRING
16. DIAPHRAGM HOUSING SCREW (4)
17. DIAPHRAGM HOUSING
18. WASHER
19. SPACER
20. DIAPHRAGM
21. IDLE SCREW LIMITER CAP
22. IDLE MIXTURE SCREW
23. SPRING
24. THROTTLE BODY
25. BODY FLANGE SCREW (3)
26. THROTTLE SHAFT ARM
27. PUMP CONNECTOR LINK
28. BODY GASKET
29. FAST IDLE CAM
30. FAST IDLE CAM SCREW
31. MAIN BODY
32. DISCHARGE BALL
33. DISCHARGE BALL WEIGHT
34. METERING ROD JET
35. LOW SPEED JET
36. FLOAT
37. FLOAT PIN
38. NEEDLE PIN
39. NEEDLE SPRING
40. NEEDLE, NEEDLE SEAT, GASKET
41. CHOKE CONNECTOR ROD
42. CHOKE CONNECTOR ROD RETAINER
43. METERING ROD
44. AIR HORN GASKET
45. AIR HORN

Exploded drawing of a carburetor with callouts.

the element is of the oiled-foam type, it is reuseable by cleaning it in a solvent and then squeezing it out dry before reoiling it.

As for the disposable element, it can be cleaned, if it's not too dirty, by blowng out with compressed air. Before you stick the element in the housing, take a clean cloth and wipe carefully the inside of the filter housing to remove any dirt, oil deposits, or other particles that could find their way into the carburetor. Put the filter in, the top on and screw the wing nut down. Replace the air filter at frequent intervals if you drive under very dusty conditions.

For the carburetor to work well, it must receive a clean, unrestricted supply of air. Replacing a dirty air filter element is simple: remove the top of the housing and lift out the old element. (Also explained in text.)

Screws holding carburetor together are tightened.

THE CARBURETOR

First off, don't get the idea that you have to disassemble the carburetor to maintain it. In fact, if the carburetor is working well, that is, the engine starts easily, doesn't stumble during acceleration, delivers good mileage and idles smoothly, *leave it alone*.

This device is a complex atomizer or rather, a group of atomizers. At idle, one of them is working. Another, called the accelerator pump, squirts for a moment when you move the accelerator, and a third spritzer handles medium speeds. Most current cars have a fourth atomizer that works only from ¾ to full throttle.

On top of all this and just below the air cleaner is the choke which thermostatically controls the air flow when the engine is cold. Directly linked to the operation of the choke is the fast idle cam. This is a notched or stepped piece of metal, usually linked to the choke by a rod that catches a tab or screw that holds the throttle open slightly while the engine is warming up.

The last major component of the carburetor is a gasoline reservoir with a float controlled needle valve not unlike a toilet flush tank.

A couple of other items that modern carburetors have are the anti-stall dashpot and the idle-speed solenoid.

The dashpot is a small, donut-shaped mechanism mounted on the side of the carburetor. It consists of a spring-and-diaphragm construction that activates a rod resting against the throttle linkage. The purpose of the dashpot is to let the throttle valve close slowly, reducing noxious emissions when the gas pedal is released.

The dashpot is adjusted by a threaded stem or threaded mounting on the diaphragm. As with all major adjustments, you should consult a service manual for your particular car and engine.

Shows an in-line fuel filter with a vent tube alongside the fuel line from the gas tank. Explained in text.

Similar in function to the dashpot is the idle-speed solenoid or throttle modulator. Its job is to stop all gas flow in the carburetor when the ignition is turned off, to keep the engine from continuing to run on, or "diesel." Dieseling refers to an engine running without spark to ignite the fuel. Emission controls tend to make internal engine temperature high enough to make any carbon deposits in the cylinders white hot. This in turn is hot enough to burn the fuel drawn into the cylinder in the moment after you've switched off but before the engine stops turning.

FUEL FILTERS

Although it's a small, simple looking item, the fuel filter plays an important role in the fuel system. It must trap dirt and water before they get into the carburetor.

Fuel filters can be found in the inlet side of the carburetor, in the fuel pump, or somewhere along the gas line between the fuel pump and the carburetor. Other locations can be in the fuel line from the fuel pump to the gas tank and in the gas tank itself at the end of the pickup tube. Your shop manual should indicate where it is and what type (disposable or reuseable).

FUEL PUMP

The fuel pump is the "heartbeat" of the fuel system, as its pumping or pulsating action draws gas from the tank and feeds it to the carburetor.

There are two basic kinds of fuel pumps: mechanical and electric.

The mechanical pump is the most common type. Mounted on the engine, it contains a lever or rod that flexes a diaphragm and an inlet and outlet valve. Mechanical fuel pumps go bad because their diaphragms rupture. But as a rule, they are reliable and can perform for many thousands of miles. If a rupture does occur, it will let oil in the crankcase escape through the pump's vent hole.

Most modern mechanical fuel pumps are not rebuildable. When they go bad, they must be replaced.

Removing a mechanical pump is relatively simple: all that you need do is to disconnect the fuel lines and undo two cap-screws holding the pump onto the block.

But, take care when installing a new pump. Compare the new pump with the old

72

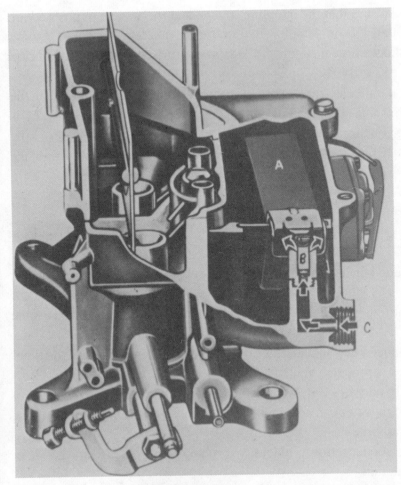

CARBURETOR
A. Float Leveler
B. Float Valve
C. Gas Inlet From Fuel Pump

one in every way. Make sure that the mounting flange and rocker arm or pushrod are identical. Although the job is simple, the cramped quarters of some engine compartments can make it a little difficult. So, don't be surprised if you skin a knuckle or two.

Now, if your car has an electric fuel pump, chances are it will be mounted on the firewall or near the gas tank. This type of pump starts working as soon as the key is turned on, even before you turn it all the way to the start position. You'll hear a clicking sound. That's the pump filling the line to the carburetor and the reservoir. Wait until the clicking gets very slow before firing up the engine.

THE GAS TANK

Before we conclude our little tour of the fuel system, let's take a look at the gas tank.

Because it's out of sight, we don't pay much attention to it, but it needs some looking after, too.

The best maintenance you can undertake for the tank is to keep it full all the time, and to make sure that it's properly vented.

With the tank only partially full, water from condensation forms on the walls of the tank. In time, enough water can accumulate to not only rust the tank but also plug up the fuel filters or carburetor.

To minimize the condensation problem, every so often pour a "dry gas", or cleaner solvent into the tank.

If the air vent in the tank (sometimes in the cap) gets clogged, the car acts as though it has run out of gas even though you have plenty. So there's very little you have to do to your fuel system besides change filters and look at it once in a while, but it is important and you will be rewarded with better mileage and performance.

74

Chapter 11

YOUR ELECTRICAL SYSTEM

Electricity in the modern car runs the lights, windshield wipers, heating and air conditioning, blowers, radio, window lifts, gauges, warning lights, buzzers and sensors for each, and on some cars seat adjustment motors, a motor to raise or lower the antenna and door and trunk lock solenoids.

The switches, fuses, relays, motors, lights, instruments and sensors are all tied together with hundreds of feet of wire. For simplicity and economy, the electrical system uses the metal of the engine, body and frame as part of the circuit. By grounding the battery with a short cable to the nearest engine or frame metal, it is possible to use just a single wire from the battery to each component.

The circuit is completed through the attachment points of each component or, if that's not possible, as in the case of a light fixture, mounted on a fiber glass panel. It's done by using another short length of wire to the nearest chassis metal.

A major wire comes from the battery to the fuse box and connects to some of the fuses and to some of the switches. The fused lines then go to switches, relays, solenoids (all are switches) or to components that have their switches on their ground side. The layout of the circuit is determined by the location of the component, the location of the switch, how far apart they are and the quantity of current necessary to operate the component. Wire absorbs current and longer wire absorbs even more. Sometimes, as in the case of the starter which needs the most electricity, a solenoid (electrically activated switch) is put right next to the component. This way a small low-

75

This starter has the solenoid affixed to it. When the solenoid becomes energized when the key is turned on, the plunger A is drawn into the solenoid, which causes the starter gear (B) to engage with the flywheel ring gear, to spin the engine into life. (Courtesy Prestolite .)

amp switch on the dash can control a high-amp circuit without long lengths of heavy wire lowering the amperage.

Electrical problems seem mysterious, but are really well within the ability of a novice trouble-shooter by simply using the wiring diagrams in the shop service manual. Having a mechanic find the reason a good bulb in a circuit with a good fuse won't burn is usually quite expensive because the search takes time. All the mechanic is doing is looking at the connection points to make sure they are secure, not corroded, and then, if the connection points are not at fault, the mechanic looks at the full length of the wire to find the break. It's easy to follow the wire because the diagram shows exactly the color or colors of the insulation. Each color or combination is used for one specific purpose.

Just a little bit more complicated than the general electric system is the ignition system.

Most ignition switches these days do multiple duty. When you turn the key you first unlock the steering post and send juice to the accessories. The next position activates the ignition system and the last stop activates the starter.

THE STARTER

When you turn on the ignition key, current from the battery flows through the ignition switch to the starter solenoid. The solenoid is a kind of electromagnetic switch that directs current to the starter which is a simple electric motor. At the same time, current is also flowing into the primary windings of the coil and to the breaker points which are inside the distributor.

THE DISTRIBUTOR

The distributor is the can-shaped device that has the heavy wires running out of the plastic cap, one to each spark plug and one (center) to the coil. It does just what its name implies: it distributes high voltage electricity to each spark plug wire (around the rim).

The coil is a beer-can sized transformer, receiving 12 volt current through a light wire on its rim, transforming it to over 20,000 volts and sending it out the heavy center

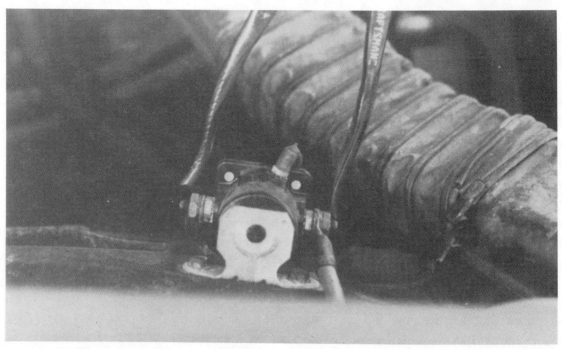

If the solenoid is believed to be bad, it can be bypassed by bridging the starter and battery terminals with a heavy jumper cable or a large pair of pliers.

To bypass a suspectedly faulty ignition switch at the solenoid, bridge the battery terminal and the ignition switch terminal on the solenoid with an object like a screwdriver.

wire. This wire goes in the center of the distributor cap under which is a rotating finger which points the current at the correct spark plug wire. Timing is all important here and is accomplished by opening the points at precisely the moment the piston reaches a given place in the cylinder. (The 20,000 volt current is not continuous.) It happens only when the low voltage circuit is interrupted. The points are part of the low voltage circuit and are opened by a cam on the shaft just below the rotor finger.

Hooked up to the points is a little metal cylinder called a condenser. Its purpose is to store electricity that would otherwise jump the gap between the points when they opened and cause them to burn or "pit."

In the case of the newer, electronic ignitions, there are no points. And, in place of the rotor that is used in conventional ignition systems, there's a spoke-shaped wheel that triggers a solid state sensor assembly.

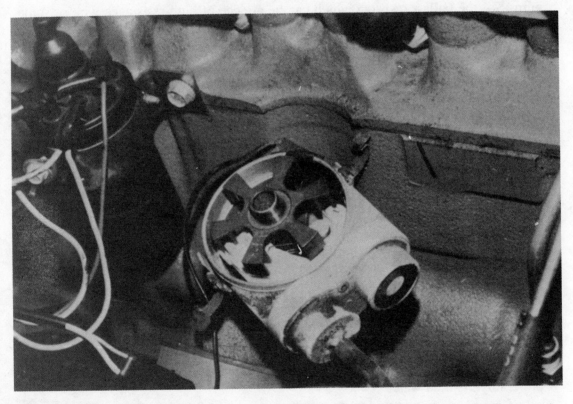

In place of the points and condenser, as found in a conventional ignition system, the distributor in an electronic-ignition setup contains a "spoke shaped" wheel called a trigger wheel. Explained in text.

There are other electrical components that come into play to control current throughout the systems.

One such device is called the voltage regulator. Its job is to limit or regulate the current that the alternator (or generator on older cars) produces and sends to the battery. If the voltage regulator goes on the blink, the battery can discharge itself through the regulator. Also, the alternator can send too much voltage to the battery and overcharge it.

Another little item that is incorporated in the starting and ignition systems is a ballast resistor. It comes into play, after the engine has started, and lowers voltage going to the primary windings in the coil and to the points.

When an engine is first being started, it needs maximum voltage to produce a hot spark to get things going. But once the engine has started, the voltage going to the primary windings and the points doesn't need to be that high, or else the points will burn. So, the ballast resistor, which can be a piece of high-resistance wire or some switching device, cuts in when the ignition key is let go to slow down or "weaken" the current.

A sure sign of a defective resistor is the engine dying immediately after the engine has started and the key let go.

THE BATTERY

Now that you've seen how the current gets to the engine, let's be more specific about keeping the juice moving.

Your battery is the heart of the electric system and there are a few things you can do to keep it reliable and extend its life.

The two most common chores you can undertake are maintaining the electrolyte level and keeping the cable clamps tight on their posts and free of corrosion.

Water must be added to the cells occasionally (unless it's one of the newest sealed-type batteries) especially during hot weather. Evaporation of the electrolyte's water content can also occur when a voltage regulator acts up and overcharges the battery. And, it's worth mentioning that only water should be added to the cells, preferably distilled water.

Corrosion is something that you have to be on guard for because it can impede the flow of current from the battery. If it gets too severe, it'll put the battery out of circuit

80

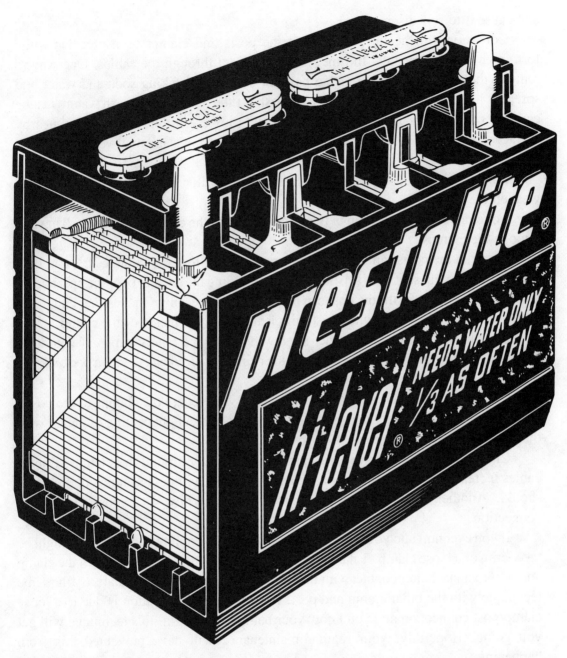

This cutaway shows the inner construction of a typical automotive battery. The plates in the cells are "sandwiched" together with separators between the plates to prevent short-circuiting. Access to the cells for adding water is provided by the cell caps on top.

and cause it to self-discharge.

Corrosion will accumulate around the posts and clamps as a greenish-white formation of acid crystals. In time, it will eat right through the cables. One way to remove those deposits is to make a paste or solution of baking soda and water and spread it liberally on the deposits. Next, wash off the battery with fresh water. Just be careful not to get carried away and let the acid (however diluted) get on any nearby surfaces. And, do make sure the cell caps are snugged down and their vent holes taped shut.

If any baking soda finds its way into the cells, it will neutralize the electrolyte and weaken the battery.

To remove corrosion from between the posts and the cable clamps, you'll have to remove the clamps.

To clean the posts, an inexpensive, post-cleaning tool is available. It's a hollow metal cylinder with stiff wire bristles inside. By sliding the cleaner over the post and by twisting is back and forth, the post can be cleaned quite easily. On the other end of the tool will be found a small wire brush for cleaning out the inside of the clamp.

Alternatives to the post cleaner are a wire brush and emery paper. If you don't have a regular cleaning tool, the inside of the clamp can be cleaned with a pocket knife or similar tool.

Once all traces of corrosion have been removed, secure the clamps to the posts, making sure they fit tightly for good contact, then smear a light coating of grease over them to inhibit any recurrence of corrosion.

Check carefully for frayed cable strands especially around the clamps. Frayed cables increase the electrical resistance and the cable can't pass as much current as it should. Another cause of high resistance to current flow is a loose clamp/post connection.

If you ever hop into your car, turn on the key and...nothing happens, you might be the victim of a loose clamp. Take a screwdriver and jam the tip of it between the clamp and post to make better contact with them. If the engine still doesn't start, try the same technique with the other clamp and post. If your non-start situation is due to a loose clamp/post connection and you know your battery is all right, this technique will get you going. Hopefully, your regular maintenance will have prevented this from happening.

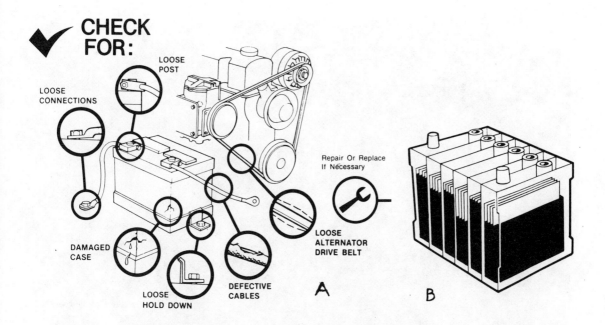

CHECK FOR:

LOOSE POST

LOOSE CONNECTIONS

Repair Or Replace If Necessary

LOOSE ALTERNATOR DRIVE BELT

DAMAGED CASE

LOOSE HOLD DOWN

DEFECTIVE CABLES

A

B

Drawing (A) shows some common battery problems. In drawing (B), you see what happens when the electrolyte solution gets too low: the tops of the plates become exposed to air and can harden, thereby losing their capacity to generate electricity.

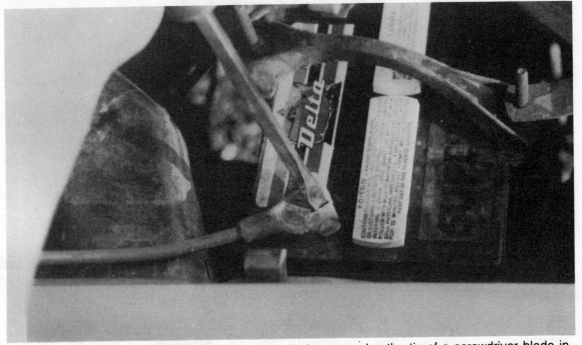

To determine if the battery's cable clamp is loose, wedge the tip of a screwdriver blade in between the clamp and the post, while having the engine cranked over.

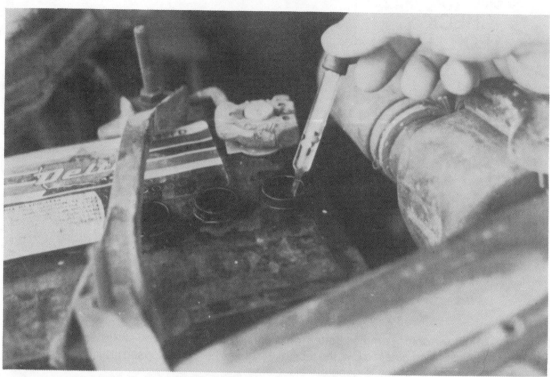

An inexpensive hydrometer provides a quick means to determine a battery's state of charge. The number of balls that float in the tube indicate a cell's strength.

This exploded drawing of an alternator shows that it's of relatively simple construction. Little maintenance is needed with the alternator, other than making sure the driving belt is tensioned properly and the wire connections to it are tight and clean. (Courtesy Prestolite)

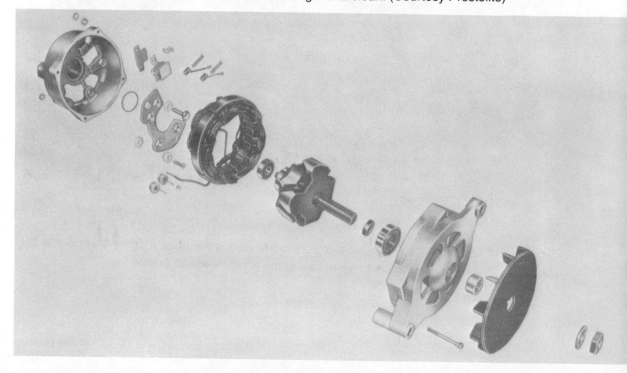

THE ALTERNATOR

The battery must be kept charged in some way so that it will be able to start the engine.

That brings us to the alternator which is an A.C. generator driven by the engine. Older cars had D.C. generators. But, since alternators are more widespread on modern cars, we'll confine our facts to them. The alternator is more efficient at lower engine speeds than the old generator.

There's not that much involved in alternator maintenance, other than making sure the driving belt to the alternator is properly tensioned. This belt usually drives the water pump (to which the fan is bolted) and sometimes the power steering pump.

If the belt is too loose, the belt will slip and not spin the alternator fast enough to generate electricity. And, if the belt is too tight, the bearings in the alternator and water pump will fail prematurely, due to overloading.

A rule-of-thumb measurement for correct belt tension is to push down on the belt with your finger midway between the pulleys that the belt rides on. The belt should have about ½ to ¾-inch of play. To adjust tension, slacken the bolts or nuts securing the alternator to its mounting brackets and reposition the alternator. It's a simple procedure.

Before you decide to adjust that old belt, inspect it closely for wear, glazed surfaces, oil deposits, and cracking. It's false economy to keep an old or worn belt in the hopes of saving a few dollars.

Drive belts can be kept pliant and longer wearing by spraying them with a silicone preservative.

Like other electrical components, make sure all the wires to the alternator are tight and clean.

If the alternator can't keep the battery charged, or if the voltage regulator malfunctions, the alternator "warning" light will come on. If the ALT light flickers on, such as would occur at low engine speeds, the battery may be run down. Check the battery posts and clamps for corrosion and loose mountings which cause high resistance to current flow.

But, if the ALT light flickers on and off at all speeds, and the battery runs down, first check the fan belt tension. If it's tight then have the voltage regulator checked. This component controls the voltage from the alternator, and when the engine isn't

85

running, the regulator breaks the circuit to keep the battery from draining back through the system. Modern voltage regulators are usually sealed units and can't be repaired. Well, there's the description. Now on to the ignition system.

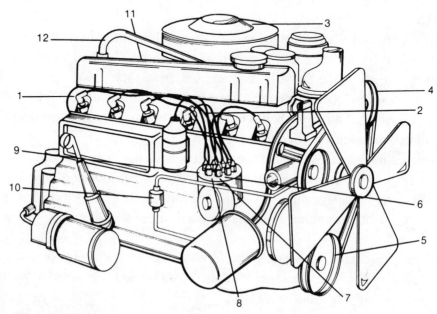

Use This Handy
Tune Up Check-List

1. Spark Plugs
2. Spark Plug Leads
3. Air Filter
4. Battery Charging Systems

5. Timing*
6. Distributor Cap
7. Distributor Rotor
8. Points*

9. Condenser*
10. Fuel Filter
11. Heat Riser Valve
12. PCV System

*In conventional systems.

This illustration shows the location of various components on an engine that may require attention during a tune-up.

Chapter 12

YOUR IGNITION SYSTEM AND HOW TO TUNE IT

THE COIL

We've described the ignition switch. A wire runs from it to one of the small terminals of the coil. Inside the coil it wraps around an iron bar a number of times, making the iron bar an electromagnet. Still inside the coil, a second wire is wound many times around the first or primary winding. By applying a well known but still mysterious characteristic of electromagnetism, a second current of much higher voltage is created in the secondary winding. 12 volts go in one place and 30,000 volts come out another—but just for a moment. The secondary current is induced only at the moment the primary current is shut off. But that's okay. This high voltage is needed at the spark plug for only a fraction of a second.

BREAKER POINTS AND CONDENSER

Back to the first wire (primary winding) wrapped around the bar. It comes out of the coil via the second small terminal on the coil and goes to the condenser and the breaker points. The breaker is the switch that shuts off the primary current thereby activating the secondary circuit. Most of the time the current flows through the breaker points to ground, and the flow would make it difficult to open the points if it had no optional route. So we give the current an optional path—the condenser. This lets us shut off the primary circuit, that is, open the points, quickly, neatly, (no sparking) and with precise timing. All of these characteristics are necessary to making that brief high voltage blast when and what we want it to be. We want it long. About 80 microseconds. That's eighty millionths of a second. We also need it between 1,400 and 24,000 times a minute. Which is all to say that there must be great precision in the operation of this system.

Look for carbon tracks inside the distributor cap, inspect the spark plug contacts inside the cap for corrosion and pitting. Same goes for the center contact that directs high-tension current from the coil to the rotor (shown by pointing pen).

THE DISTRIBUTOR

Accuracy is needed within the ignition system and in meshing the system with the mechanical (pistons, valves, crankshaft) and fuel systems. This accuracy is achieved by interlocking the control functions in one unit, the distributor, and gearing it directly to the crankshaft. Inside the distributor a shaft runs at exactly half engine speed. Cam lobes on the shaft push open the breaker points. High voltage wires from the spark plugs and coil come together in the distributor cap. The inside of the cap has a terminal for each wire, the coil wire in the center and the plug wires around the perimeter. The rotor

88

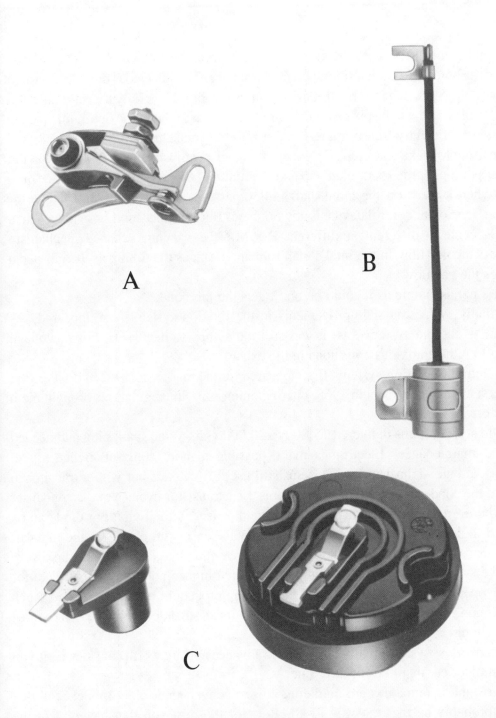

A

B

C

Here you see the basic components of a distributor in a conventional ignition system. A-points; B-condenser; C-two types of rotors. The parts are normally replaced during a major tune-up.

on the end of the distributor shaft takes the current from the coil wire terminal and as it turns, distributes it to each terminal on the perimeter. The juice goes down the wire to the spark plug and, eager to be grounded, jumps the gap. Hopefully the valve, set the gas in, then closed, so the piston could compress the gas and is at the optimum place in its cycle to efficiently transmit a terrific push to the crankshaft.

In order to make and keep all this activity precise, adjustments can be made to the breaker point gap, the spark plug gap and the timing, which refers to each spark plug firing when a mark on the crankshaft pulley passes a degree in its 360 degree of rotation. One other control device is at work here. Because the "optimum place" in a piston's cycle is different at different R.P.M., the vacuum advance mechanism monitors the gas flow in the intake manifold and changes the timing as the gas pedal changes the gas flow.

It's not as simple as it could be but it gets the job done.

Finally, some major improvements in the ignition system have appeared. As accurate as the old system was, it was still too sloppy to handle the higher voltage needed to reduce noxious emissions in the exhaust.

Electronic ignition systems first appeared on the market in 1962 and were first used as standard equipment in 1968, but tightening emission regulations brought them to the fore in 1972-73.

Old style systems delivered 15,000 to 20,000 volts to the spark plug and needed frequent maintenance. Electronics make possible a more constant higher (up to 32,000) voltage. Transistorized systems still use the breaker, but with a transitor in place of the condenser. Breaker-less systems use a transistor in place of the condenser and either a magnetic pulse and magnetic field sensor, a light emitting diode and a infrared light sensor or a non-magnetic metal sensor in place of the breaker mechanism. (Sensors, diodes and transistors are solid state devices and make very sensitive switches, relays etc.) This permits much higher voltages which make for cleaner operation; eliminates most of the tune-up procedure because these no-touch systems don't wear and, spark plugs, the only parts left that do wear, last two to three times as long.

Breakerless systems really are a terrific advance and are worth considering if you have an older car that doesn't have one.

Most auto companies are marketing kits to convert their older models and that would probably be the best way to go. But, for those of you that haven't got the electronic system yet, we'll tell you how to tune it.

90

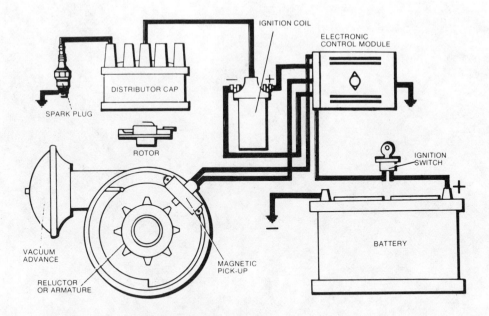

IGNITION COIL

ELECTRONIC
CONTROL MODULE

DISTRIBUTOR CAP

SPARK PLUG

ROTOR

IGNITION
SWITCH

+

VACUUM
ADVANCE

MAGNETIC
PICK-UP

RELUCTOR
OR ARMATURE

BATTERY

Conventional Ignition System

▭ STARTING CIRCUIT
▬ RUN CIRCUIT
▦ SECONDARY IGNITION SYSTEM

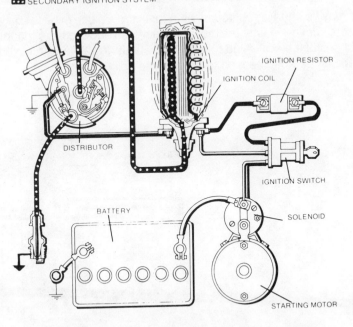

IGNITION RESISTOR

IGNITION COIL

DISTRIBUTOR

IGNITION SWITCH

BATTERY

SOLENOID

STARTING MOTOR

Components in an electronic-ignition system.

To see if the points may be shorting out, open them (or insert a piece of paper between them) and rest the shaft of a screwdriver against the movable point arm and the base mounting plate. Then place the distributor end of the coil's high-tension lead about ⅛ to ¼-inch from some metal part of the engine.If a spark jumps from the lead to ground, the points are bad.

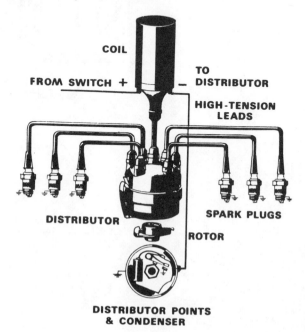

TUNING THE IGNITION

Tuning up an engine may involve only cleaning and adjusting the spark plugs and breaker points, or it may necessitate that new plugs, points, condensor, distributor cap, rotor, etc., all be replaced.

The condition of these items will determine if they should be replaced or not.

We'll assume that it's been quite some time since the last major tune-up. So, we'll replace all the major components in the ignition system and check the timing of the engine, too.

Right at the outset, though, you should realize that if an engine is worn out, no amount of tuning is going to bring it up to peak performance. We will assume here that that is not the case.

To remove and replace spark plugs, you're going to need the right tools. They will include a ratchet wrench and a deep socket. Get a socket that has a padded insert that will grip the plug and hold it while it's being removed. When removing the plug cables, don't jerk them off; wiggle the boot and lift off gently. And, it's a good idea to mark each cable so it won't be placed on the wrong plug later and cause misfiring.

Once you've removed the plugs, examine their firing ends for clues as to what's going on inside the combustion chambers. The spark plugs are ''electrical barometers'', so to speak; they'll tell you a lot about an engine's operating condition.

But, you have to learn how to interpret the color of the electrodes, insulators and deposits.

For instance, when the engine is in good condition and combustion favorable, the outer electrode and shell will have a grayish appearance, while the center electrode and insulator nose will be tan colored.

If the firing end of the plug is covered with black fluffy deposits it means that the plug is too cold for the particular driving conditions to which you subject your car. In this case, a hotter plug is needed to burn deposits away. If only one or two of the plugs are carbon-fouled, it could be due to burned or badly worn valves in the cylinder(s).

Should the plugs have shiny black deposits, it means that excessive oil is getting into the cylinders past the rings.

When the electrodes are severely worn and the nose insulator of the plug has a white, blistered appearance, it means that the plug is running too hot and needs to be replaced with a colder-operating type. An extreme example of a spark plug being subjected to too much heat is when the electrodes have melted. This condition would

93

Carbon Fouled

Carbon fouled plugs show dry fluffy black depos
which may result from over-rich carburetion, ove
choking, a stocking manifold heat valve or clogg
air cleaner. Faulty breaker points, weak coil
condenser, worn ignition cables can redu
voltage and cause misfiring. Excessive idlin
slow speeds under light load also can keep pl
temperatures so low that normal combusti
deposits are not burned off. In such a case a hott
type spark plug will better resist carbon deposit

Oil Fouled

Wet oily deposits may be caused by oil leakir
past worn piston rings. "Break-in" of a new
overhauled engine before rings are fully seate
may also produce this condition. A porous vacuu
booster pump diaphragm or excessive valve ste
guide clearances can also cause oil foulin
Usually these plugs can be degreased, cleane
and reinstalled. While hotter type spark plugs w
reduce oil-fouling, an engine overhaul may b
necessary to correct this condition.

Burned Electrodes

Burned or blistered insulator nose and bad
eroded electrodes are indications of spark plu
overheating. Improper spark timing or low octan
fuel can cause detonation and overheating. Lea
air fuel mixtures, cooling system stoppages c
sticking valves may also result in this conditior
Sustained high-speed, heavy-load service ca
produce high temperatures which require use c
colder spark plugs.

be caused by pre-ignition, which is an irregular form of combustion where the fuel and air charge is ignited prematurely due to abnormally high operating conditions inside the combustion chamber.

Even if the plugs are of the correct type and the engine is operating within normal conditions, deposits will form on the electrodes as natural by-products of combustion. The many kinds of additives used in today's fuels and oils will result in brown, yellow, or white deposits forming on the firing ends.

If the plugs don't have excessive electrode wear, the deposits can be cleaned off by either sandblasting them or by soaking them in solvent and cleaning them with a wire brush.

There are two things you must consider about spark plugs when replacing them: they must be of the correct heat range and of the proper reach. The heat range is the capacity by which a spark plug dissipates heat. It's determined by the length of the insulator nose. A short-length nose means the plug is a "cold" type and will get rid of heat more slowly than the cold plug.

Be sure to check the manufacturer's recommendations concerning what heat range of plug to use. If you drive your car around town at low-operating speeds, you may want to use a slightly hotter plug than standard to burn off the combustion products that will form.

Conversely, for higher-speed driving, a colder plug may help due to the higher temperatures generated by the engine.

As for reach, it's the length of the threaded portion of the plug that screws into the cylinder. Use only a plug with the same reach as the plugs you take out.

Although spark plugs are pre-gapped during manufacture, you should check them with a gauge according to maker's specs. Incidentally, if you measure the gaps on plugs that have been in service for some time, use a wire gauge, not a feeler gauge. A wire gauge will provide a more accurate reading, due to the pits on the electrodes. A flat feeler gauge will rest on top of the sides of the pits and give a false reading.

When installing the plugs, make sure there are new gasket washers, unless the spark plugs are of the tapered seat design in which case no washers are used.

After the plug has been snugged down into the hole, make one-quarter turn with the wrench to seat the plug. If you over-tighten, you'll damage the plug; if you don't tighten it enough, you'll cause a loss of cylinder compression to occur.

Installing points is perhaps the most difficult (at first) part of a tune-up. This is especially true if the distributor is inaccessible to begin with. But once you change

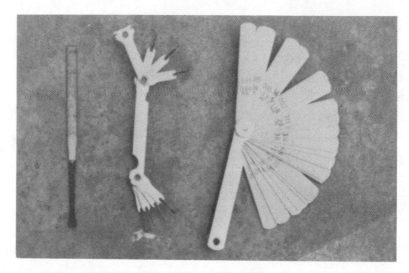

For tuning up the ignition system, these tools are a must: points dressing file; spark plug gap-measuring wire gauges; and flat feeler gauges for adjusting the gap between the points.

Point gap is measured when the high spot, or lobe, of the breaker cam is pushing against the rubbing block of the movable-point arm to separate the contacts. A flat feeler gauge (arrow) of the proper thickness is then inserted between the contacts and the gap adjusted by means of a screw or by moving the fixed point after it's been loosened.

points a couple of times, it becomes easier to do. After you remove the distributor cap and rotor, the points can be removed by taking out two screws and disconnecting the condenser wire to the point assembly. If the condenser is separate from the point assembly, it'll have its own securing screw. Some points and condensers are all one unit, which simplifies their removal and installation.

Note: On cars with a windshield antenna, there may be a radio-interference shield around the point assembly that must be removed before the points can be taken out. A couple of screws are all that holds it in place.

Installing new points and condenser isn't all that difficult, although the first time or two you undertake it you'll feel all thumbs. What is critical, however, is setting the point gap. The gap setting for your particular engine will be in the owner's manual. To set the gap, you'll have to turn the engine over so that the lobe, or high spot of the breaker cam, is resting against the rubbing block on the moveable point.

Then with either turning an eccentric adjusting screw located near the point (the gap-adjusting screw will usually be smaller than the locking screw that secures the fixed point to the backing plate) or a slot for a screwdriver to fit, the gap can be set. By sticking the tip of the screwdriver in a slot or notch, and twisting it, the fixed point can be adjusted.

The most-precise way to adjust point gap is to use a dwellmeter.

Dwellmeters usually incorporate a tachometer, too, for registering engine rpm (revolutions per minute). It's easy to use a dwellmeter; all that's required to hook it up is to attach one lead to the minus terminal of the coil and hook the other lead to a good ground on the engine. Here again, you'll have to obtain the manufacturer's specs for your particular engine.

After you've taken a dwell reading, you may have to adjust the point gap some-what to obtain a precise reading. This can be an irksome process until you get it right. Instead of adjusting the gap with feeler gauges, you may have a distributer setup where point gap can be set with the engine running by using an Allen wrench inserted into a corresponding screw on the point assembly.

Many modern cars have a "window" on the side of their distributors which provides entry for an Allen wrench. With the dwellmeter hooked up and the engine running, it's just a matter of turning the wrench either direction until the dwell reading is on spot.

Once you've set the dwell, next comes the matter of checking the engine's timing, with a timing light.

97

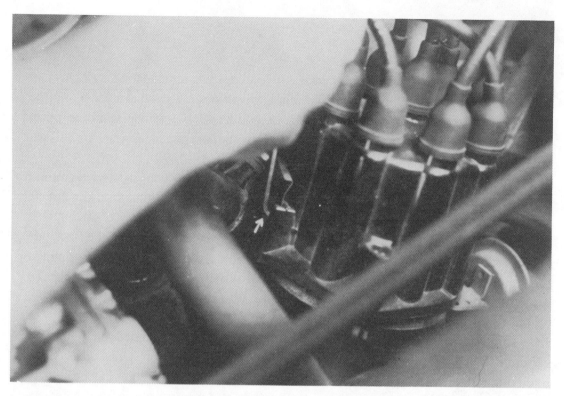

In this design distributor, an Allen wrench is used to adjust point gap by being inserted into a special screw located in the point assembly. Access is possible by raising a "window" on side of distributor.

Another, more precise way to set the points' gap is to use the dwellmeter, a device which measures the number of degrees the points remain closed as the breaker cam rotates. The reading for this particular engine (a V8 is 31 degrees.)

What do we mean by timing, anyway?

It takes a certain amount of time for the fuel to burn.

Because of this, ignition must occur when the piston is a certain distance from the top of its stroke. By the time the full pressure of the charge has been generated, the piston has already moved up to the top of its stroke (top Dead Center) and started back down.

If the spark occurs too early, the burning charge will exert its full force while the piston is still rising. And, if the spark happens too late, then the piston will have gone too far down the bore and little pressure will be exerted against it.

Now at idling or low speeds, the charge has time to burn; so the spark has to take place relatively "late," or when the piston is near the top of its compression stroke. But at higher speeds, the piston is traveling much faster, and there isn't that much time to utilize the burning charge. So, the spark must occur earlier.

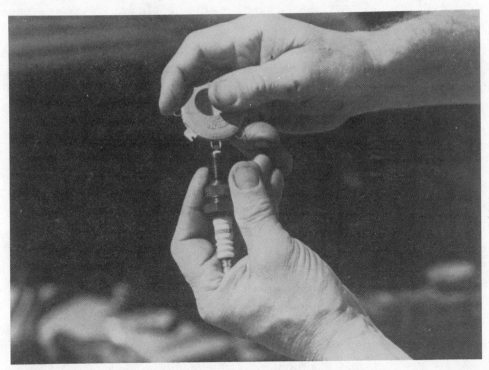

Use a special wire gauge to set the electrode gap on spark plugs. Don't use a flat feeler gauge, as it won't give an accurate reading if there is any pitting on the electrodes.

Spark advance and retard are automatically controlled by a vacuum diaphragm on the side of the distributor and/or by a centrifugal advance (spring-loaded weights inside the distributor).

You're now ready to time the engine. If your timing light is operated by the engine, hook up the two battery leads and the remaining wire to the number one spark plug.

Your owner's service manual will tell you which cylinder is number one, that is, the one that fires first.

Some timing lights run off house current. Regardless which type light you have, just make sure that you hook it up to the number-one cylinder.

After you've hooked up the light, locate the timing marks on the crankshaft pulley and the reference point on the timing-gear cover.

They might be difficult to see, so you might want to outline the marks with chalk or white paint. The next step is to check the owner's or service manual for the number of degrees of spark advance. Each engine has a different figure, so be sure to check for your engine.

If a figure of 8-10 degrees is given, adjust for the higher reading. When the timing is spot on, the reference pointer on the gear cover should be directly opposite the 10-degree mark on the crankshaft pulley, as the timing light "freezes" their motion. The timing light is operated by the current pulsations of the spark plug as it fires. So the flashes coincide with the rpm of the crankshaft pulley marks to make them appear as though they're standing still.

After you've installed new points or cleaned and adjusted the old ones, it's doubtful if the timing will be spot on. So that means you have to adjust the distributor housing to make the points open either later, or earlier, depending on which way the timing is off.

To change the timing, all that you will have to do is to loosen the pinch bolt that holds the distributor in place and then rotate the distributor in either direction until the correct mark lines up with the reference pointer. Tighten the bolt and hook up the vacuum line to the diaphragm unit.

After the timing has been set, you can adjust the carburetor idle and mixture screws according to factory specifications.

Many new cars today incorporate electronic ignition. Since there are a variety of types we won't cover them here. Your service manual will have the most accurate information about it.

Suffice it to say that the timing can be set in the same manner as conventional ignition using a dwellmeter and timing light.

Because of the high-voltage current to the spark plugs, don't substitute conventional plug wires for the electronic spark plug cables. They won't handle the increased voltage for very long.

As you've seen from the previous pages, there's quite a bit to the electrical side of the engine. At first it seems confusing. But with a little patience and practice, you'll be undertaking your own tune-ups and enjoying it.

So, as soon as you finish lining up those timing marks, get set for another chapter. We still have a ways to go in helping you "double the performance of your car."

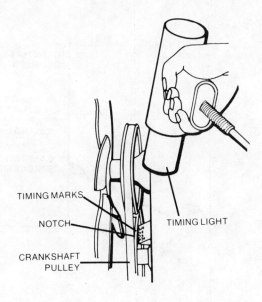

TIMING MARKS

NOTCH

TIMING LIGHT

CRANKSHAFT
PULLEY

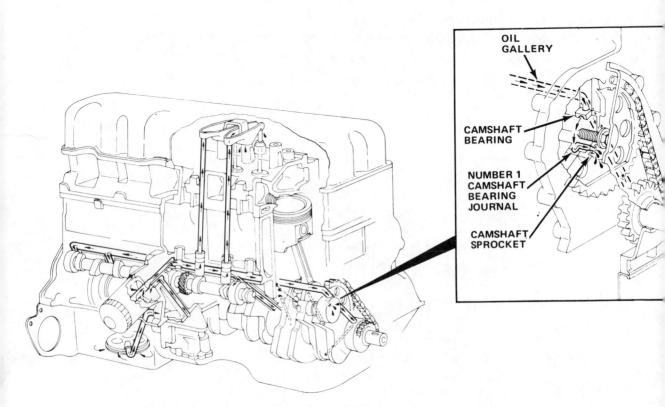

OIL
GALLERY

CAMSHAFT
BEARING

NUMBER 1
CAMSHAFT
BEARING
JOURNAL

CAMSHAFT
SPROCKET

Oil is drawn from the bottom of the engine (sump) and fed through the oil filter and lower-engine, while part of the oil flow is directed up through the cam followers, push rods and rocker arms. From there, the oil drips back down through to the oil pan, or sump, to begin the journey all over again.

Chapter 13

LUBRICATION

It's been said that an engine properly cared for should last at least 100,000 miles.

To achieve that mileage figure for your car, you should put lubrication right at the top of your necessary-maintenance list. If you change your oil regularly and keep certain other parts of the car properly lubed, you can double your car's performance by helping it to run better for a longer period of time.

Besides providing a micro-thin film of lubrication for the engine's friction-contact parts, oil has other important functions: it must also dissipate heat. Oil acts as a shock absorber too, minimizing impact forces between some components.

In the cylinders, oil has the added responsibility of sealing the very small gaps between the pistons and cylinder walls, preventing power-producing combustion gases from escaping into the crankcase.

Oil must further protect the engine's internals from rust and corrosion, plus it "collects" dirt and deposits it in the oil filter.

WHAT OIL SHOULD YOU USE?

Most oils are taken from Mother Earth and refined into two basic kinds: detergent and non-detergent. Detergent oils are recommended for most modern engines due to their high film strength, coupled with all kinds of special additives for keeping the

103

engine clean running, resistant to acids, rust, corrosion and foaming.

If you start out with a detergent oil in a new or rebuilt engine and stay with it, you'll find the engine will have minimal wear and build-up dirt, carbon, and varnish deposits.

Where detergent oil is not advisable, however, is in older, high-mileage engines that have used only non-detergent oils. Using a detergent oil in such engines will cause the dirt and carbon deposits to break loose with the result that the engine will tend to "burn," or consume large amounts of oil. What's worse, large particles of dirt or carbon will break loose and block oilways and starve the bearing surfaces in the engine of oil.

When shopping for oil, stick to popular brands and note their classifications. In other words, are they detergent or non-detergent? What kind of driving conditions are they recommended for? This information will be found somewhere on the container, usually on the top.

To ensure maximum protection for your engine with a detergent oil, make sure there are the letters MS or SE somewhere on the can. They'll tell you that the oil is suitable for extreme driving conditions and high temperatures. Considering how hot modern engines operate due to city-type driving and the modifications made to engines for emission controls, they need all the protection they can get.

If you have an older car that is driven at moderate speeds and not subjected to extreme operating conditions, you can get by with a less protective oil that has the designations MM or ML. But, remember, only a MS or SE oil will provide maximum protection.

Besides service classifications, oil is also classified according to viscosity, or "weight."

Viscosity is a measure of an oil's inherent resistance to flow. It is designated by numbers such as #10, #20, #30, etc. The higher the number, the heavier or thicker the oil. For high-temperature conditions, heavier weights of oil are necessary.

Modern oil technology has blessed the modern auto owner with multiple-viscosity oils which provide protection for an engine under a wide variety of temperature conditions. For instance, the designations 10W-30 or 20W-40 mean that such oils will provide year-round protection. The lower number indicates that during cold weather, the oil will have a lower viscosity for easy flowing, while the higher number means that the oil will not thin too much, meeting the need for a heavier oil during hot weather, high-engine-temperature conditions.

Your owner's manual will recommend certain multiple-viscosity oils for your engine.

HOW OFTEN SHOULD YOU CHANGE YOUR OIL?

The owners' manuals for new cars usually recommend oil changes every 4000 to 5000 miles. This mileage range is all right for ideal operating conditions, in which an engine can get thoroughly warmed up. But short-distance driving, especially in cold weather, is the real enemy of an engine.

Those manuals, therefore, also state that under short-distance, cold-weather conditions, the oil should be changed at 500-mile intervals, or monthly.

Now if it weren't for the water and contaminants produced by the combustion process, short-distance driving wouldn't be all that hard on an engine. But for every gallon of gas burned, nearly a gallon of water is formed as a by-product. Most of that water eventually finds its way out the exhaust pipe. But there's still enough of it that stays behind and mixes with the oil.

Although water and oil don't really mix, when they're forced under pressure throughout the engine, they emulsify, or turn into a milky solution. When this emulsion mixes with acids and varnishes, gums, and other combustion by-products, it breaks down the lubricating properties of the oil, and "eats" away at the bearing surfaces.

Continual short-trip driving doesn't allow these contaminants to burn away, so they accumulate to form a sludge.

That sludge can block oilways and filters and jam the piston rings in their grooves. Is it any wonder then that an engine will "age" prematurely?

The best protection for such conditions is to use a good MS or SE detergent oil and to change it more often than you would for normal, long-distance driving.

You can't always go by the color of the oil to tell if it needs changing, either. Detergent oils will darkent after only a few hundred miles of service. You see, the additives in detergent oil hold minute particles of soft carbon and lead in suspension. These particles are too small for the oil filter to trap; but they're harmless to the bearing surfaces.

HOW TO CHANGE YOUR OIL

One of the simplest maintenance jobs you can undertake is to change your own oil and its filter.

Considering what an engine has to contend with, it needs the protection of a good filter, along with oil changes. Some people feel that it's not necessary to change the filter every time the oil is changed. But since modern oil filters are of the full-flow type, they hold about a quart of oil. And if you don't replace it when you change the oil, that means there'll be a quart of dirty oil to contaminate the fresh supply.

All that you'll need to change the oil and filter will be a suitably sized wrench for the drain plug on the oil pan or sump, and an oil-filter wrench if your filter is the self-contained canister type.

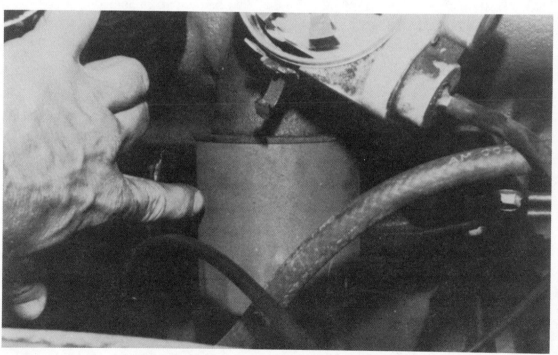

The oil filter is the canister-shaped component located on the side of six-cylinder engines. Eight-cylinder V8 engines usually have their oil filters located on the bottom.

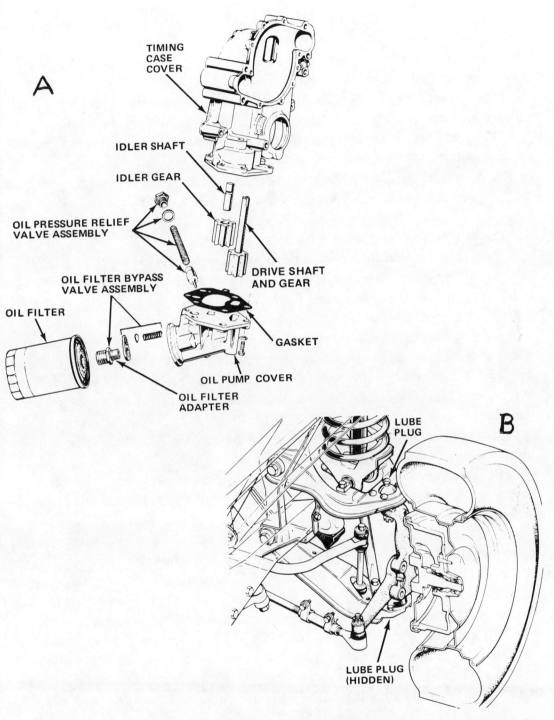

A

TIMING CASE COVER

IDLER SHAFT

IDLER GEAR

OIL PRESSURE RELIEF VALVE ASSEMBLY

OIL FILTER BYPASS VALVE ASSEMBLY

OIL FILTER

DRIVE SHAFT AND GEAR

GASKET

OIL PUMP COVER

OIL FILTER ADAPTER

B

LUBE PLUG

LUBE PLUG (HIDDEN)

Drawing A shows a view of the oil pump and oil filter, while illustration B shows the location of grease fittings on the front wheel's suspension and steering linkage.

Older type filters have a nut on the bottom of the unit so that a regular wrench will fit.

First warm the engine up, so that dirt, carbon particles, etc., are held in suspension and will exit with the oil.

Then, with a large pan underneath the drain opening area, take a wrench and remove the plug. After most of the oil has drained away, remove the filter.

Make sure the pan is underneath the filter when you unscrew it as a certain amount of oil will drain.

When installing a new filter, first smear some fresh oil on the rubber gasket to make a good seal when the filter is tightened. And, when tightening the canister type, don't use a wrench. Snug it down firmly with hand strength only. Using a wrench to tighten the filter will only make it harder to remove later.

But, do use a wrench to tighten the type and the drain plug in the oil pan!

Refill the oil supply and start the engine to let it run for a few minutes, while you check for leaks around the plug and filter.

When changing oil, don't mix detergent brands with non-detergent types as they will react by forming gum deposits and sludge.

Lubrication schedules for late model cars call for relatively infrequent greasing, but doing it more often won't hurt. Older models require a lube every 3,000 miles or every three months. If you decide to do it yourself, inexpensive, high pressure grease guns are available.

An important part of your lubrication maintenance should be that of checking the dipstick every time you fill up the gas tank.

Besides being consumed through normal service, oil loss can occur in other ways. Faulty seals, leaky gaskets, worn valve guides, piston rings, and bearings can all contribute to a diminishing oil supply.

And then there's always the PCV setup. The what? In case you're not familiar with that set of letters, it means positive crankcase ventilation. It's one of the simpler pollution-control systems on cars manufactured after 1963. The PCV system consists of a combination of hoses and check valve that takes crankcase vapors and reroutes them throught the intake manifold for burning in the combustion chambers.

The PCV valve itself has a simple construction that allows the vapors to travel only one direction. But it can get plugged up with sludge and dirt deposits, which causes a build up of pressure in the crankcase. When that happens, oil is forced out of the engine. Besides increasing oil consumption, a faulty PCV valve will make the engine run more roughly. If it's plugged up, it can be cleaned in a solvent. But considering the low price of a new PCV valve, it's better to install a new one than fool with the old one. If the PCV valve should be plugged up, better check its hose to see if it might not need attention, too.

New synthetic lubricants (non-petroleum substitutes) are available now from the major refiners. The claims made for them are quite interesting; up to ten times the useable life of regular oil; less consumption because it doesn't burn, break down or vaporize as easily, etc. Right now these synthetics cost 4 to 5 times as much as oil but last as much as ten times as long, so there seems to be a potential saving while actually getting better lubrication. Since this will make your car last longer, it could be well worth looking into. IF you decide to try this new product, it is strongly recommended that you DON'T mix a synthetic oil with your regular oil. Drain your engine thoroughly and change the filter also.

If you have lots of money and trade cars every year, you won't have to worry about a little dirty oil or what type or brand to use. But, if you're like the rest of us who must make our cars perform their best over the years, pay attention to that oil system. Your car will appreciate it by rewarding you with faithful service.

What more can you ask?

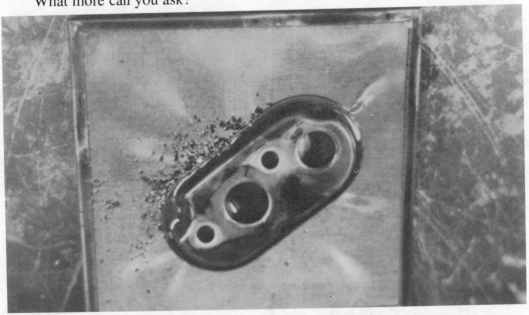

This photograph shows an automatic transmission filter after it was removed from a transmission that never had its fluid changed. Notice the wear and dirt particles that have accumulated.

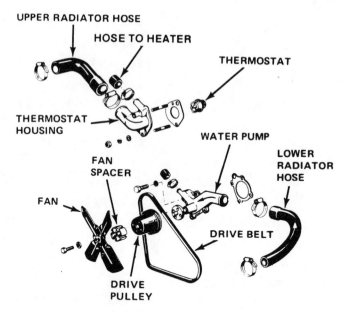

UPPER RADIATOR HOSE

HOSE TO HEATER

THERMOSTAT

THERMOSTAT HOUSING

WATER PUMP

LOWER RADIATOR HOSE

FAN SPACER

FAN

DRIVE BELT

DRIVE PULLEY

Here's an exploded view of the water pump, fan, and radiator hose assembly. Note that the hoses are held in place by special hose clamps.

A worn water pump bearing can be determined by grasping one of the fan's blades and shaking it. There should be barely any play at all, if the pump is good.

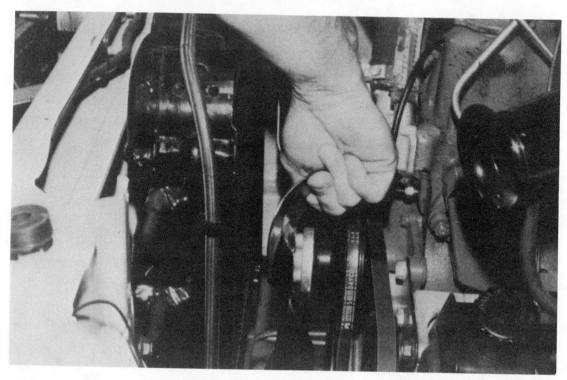

Chapter 14

YOUR COOLING SYSTEM

The performance of your car depends to a great extent on it's cooling system.

A modern engine derives its efficiency from heat. You read in the last chapter how a cold engine can hamper the lubrication of its parts. And the engine won't deliver its optimum power until the gas can vaporize enough to provide good combustion.

But heat must be kept within acceptable limits, or the engine may self-destruct from parts that over-expand and seize, such as the pistons and cylinders.

It's up to the cooling system to control the heat that the engine generates.

HOW THE COOLING SYSTEM "COOLS"

The coolant in the system is—or should be—a mixture of water and ethylene glycol (anti-freeze). We'll look at the coolant in detail later; for now we just want to see how it does its job.

The major parts of the cooling system are the radiator and cap, the hoses, the water pump and fan, the thermostat, and the hollow passages surrounding the cylinders.

Coolant is drawn from the bottom of the radiator by the water pump and forced throughout the engine's passageways, known as "jackets." These jackets surround the hottest parts of the cylinders and combustion chambers and absorb the heat from them. After the coolant circulates through the jackets, it's forced back to the top of the radiator where it filters down through the honeycomb structure of the radiator's tubes.

As the car's being driven, the flow of air through the fans and around the tubes of the radiator carries away heat. But if the engine's idling or at very low speeds, the fan must draw air in through the radiator, or else the engine would overheat.

Some fans have a clutch which disengages the fan from operation once the car reaches a certain forward speed.

The thermostat is a heat-sensitive valve located in the top, forward part of the engine, where the top radiator hose attaches to the engine.

The thermostat controls the circulation of coolant, depending on whether the engine is up to operating temperature or not. When a cold engine is started, the thermostat shuts off the flow of coolant to the radiator. In this way the coolant trapped in the jackets must recirculate through them, and, in the process, warms up much faster than if it were allowed to flow back to the radiator.

Once the engine gets warm enough, however, the thermostat opens and permits the trapped coolant to flow back to the radiator.

COOLANT

Auto makers recommend that their cars be filled with a 50/50 mixture: 50% water and 50% ethylene glycol (anti-freeze).

The primary reason for having anti-freeze in the coolant, of course, is to keep the coolant from freezing and damaging the radiator and engine. This ratio of water to ethylene glycol will give protection down to about −34 degrees F., and the glycol also helps in hot weather by raising the boiling point to 265 degrees, for the mixture.

Ethylene glycol also contains special rust and corrosion-inhibiting additives, important to the cooling system. The bearings in the water pump need it also as they get lubrication from the anti-freeze. Using plain water will shorten the life of the pump bearing.

To check the strength of the coolant, a special hydrometer is needed. Be careful when checking the radiator because the cooling system is under pressure. If the engine is very hot, protect yourself from a possible geyser of steam that could cook your hand

112

To determine the strength of the coolant (its ratio of anti-freeze to water), a special hydrometer is used. The more anti-freeze there is, the higher the float will rise in the hydrometer.

Some idea of a radiator hose's condition can be had by squeezing it together. It if feels spongy or soft, it should be replaced.

even through light gloves. Turn the cap just slightly to relieve the pressure and wait until the hissing subsides before removing the cap completely.

Also, pressure leaks in the radiator and hoses should be watched for. (Don't let the overflow tube worry you. This comes out of the radiator right at the cap, runs down the side and sometimes drips.)

Hoses should be checked periodically for soft weak spots or brittleness. Squeezing a hose will usually indicate whether it's weakened or not.

Keep the grille and radiator clear of bugs and dirt. This could lead to overheating.

Like the other systems, the cooling system needs a little regular attention.

There's no way around it.

Chapter 15

YOUR TRANSMISSION AND DRIVELINE

Now we'll follow the power from the engine through the clutch and transmission to the differential, axles and wheels.

An engine will have a limited operating range of revolutions per minute. Because of this limited operating range, your engine needs a transmission to enable you to select the right engine speed for the road conditions. The clutch is a disconnectable link between the transmission and engine. You disengage the clutch (disconnect the power) while you select a different gear. The power passes through the drive shaft into the differential, which is a gear set that is able to pass the power onto one wheel while letting the other roll freely. Differential refers to the different distances the wheels travel on opposite sides of the car while turning a corner. If the axle were solid, something would break.

THE AUTOMATIC TRANSMISSION

There are different types of automatic transmissions. Because this type of transmission is more popular on today's cars, we'll begin with it. An automatic gearbox is more complex than the standard setup—therefore it's costlier. Gas mileage isn't quite as good with an automatic, but the convenience it offers for most drivers offsets its use of more gas.

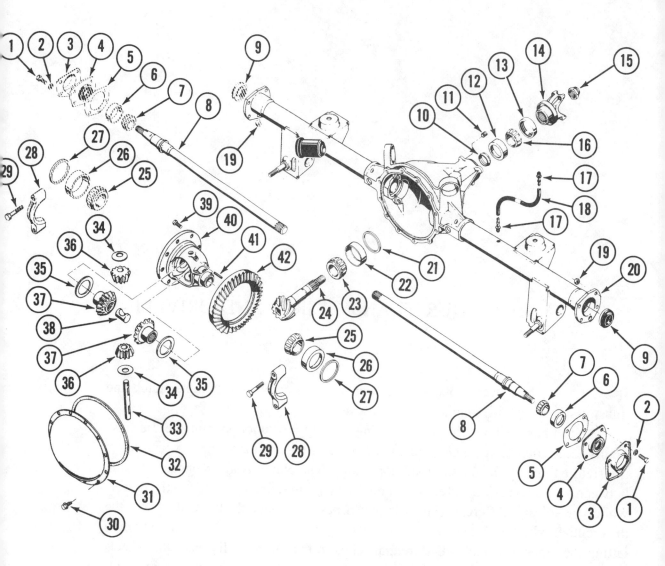

1. BOLT
2. WASHER
3. AXLE SHAFT OIL SEAL RETAINER
4. AXLE SHAFT OIL SEAL
5. AXLE SHAFT BEARING SHIM
6. AXLE SHAFT BEARING CUP
7. AXLE BEARING
8. AXLE SHAFT
9. AXLE SHAFT INNER OIL SEAL
10. PINION COLLAPSIBLE SPACER
11. FILLER PLUG
12. FRONT PINION BEARING CUP
13. PINION OIL SEAL
14. UNIVERSAL JOINT YOKE
15. PINION NUT
16. FRONT PINION BEARING
17. BREATHER
18. BREATHER HOSE
19. NUT
20. REAR AXLE HOUSING
21. DRIVE PINION DEPTH ADJUSTING SHIM

22. REAR PINION BEARING CUP
23. REAR PINION BEARING
24. DRIVE PINION
25. DIFFERENTIAL BEARING
26. DIFFERENTIAL BEARING CUP
27. DIFFERENTIAL BEARING SHIM
28. DIFFERENTIAL BEARING CAP
29. BOLT
30. BOLT
31. HOUSING COVER
32. HOUSING COVER GASKET
33. DIFFERENTIAL PINION SHAFT
34. DIFFERENTIAL PINION GEAR THRUST WASHER
35. DIFFERENTIAL SIDE GEAR THRUST WASHER
36. DIFFERENTIAL PINION GEAR
37. DIFFERENTIAL GEAR
38. DIFFERENTIAL PINION SHAFT THRUST BLOCK
39. BOLT
40. DIFFERENTIAL CASE
41. DIFFERENTIAL PINION SHAFT PIN
42. DRIVE GEAR

One of the types of automatic transmission has gears similar to a standard transmission, but in the box with the gears is one or more automatic clutches operated by varying hydraulic pressure. (This is where the power is used that cuts into your gas mileage.) Another type has a simplier gear set coupled with a torque converter. Unlike the other tansmissions which have a clutch, the torque converter does not.

Depending on engine speed, fluid is pumped into the converter, which has a series of turbine blades. At low speeds, the blades slip rather easily through the fluid and thereby transmit little torque. But as engine speed increases, the fluid becomes stiffer or offers more resistance, and becomes almost like a solid connection between the engine and the transmission.

There are other stationary blades inside the transmission that direct fluid against the driven turbine-blades to "multiply" the torque of the engine at low speeds in order to help get the car moving. To get into the intricate operation of an automatic is well beyond the scope of this chapter.

As far as maintenance is concerned, there isn't much you can do. But there are a few things you can check. One is the fluid that is so vital to the efficiency of the automatic. Only a regular automatic-transmission fluid should be used. Don't try to substitute some other lubricant in place of the fluid specified for your transmission.

You can get an idea if the transmission is healthy or not by checking the color and odor of the fluid.

The fluid's condition is checked by removing the special dipstick, which you'll find at the rear of the engine. The engine must first be warmed up to operating temperature.

Note the color and odor of the fluid. The fluid should be red. Fresh transmission fluid is pinkish, almost clear. If the fluid is milky or brown in appearance, it could be an indication of trouble. Smell the fluid. If it emits a burnt odor, better get your set of wheels down to the local transmission specialist.

The fluid should be changed every 25,000 miles whether it looks okay or not. It operates under a lot of pressure and heat and is bound to undergo some breakdown.

If you detect any noises or peculiar behavior in the transmission, considering how expensive transmission overhauls are, don't hesitate in taking your car to a transmission specialist. If it slips under load, sticks in one gear, or slips in one gear and not another gear, or won't kick into passing gear, have it looked at. Sometimes just adjusting the bands or shift/linkage will cure a problem.

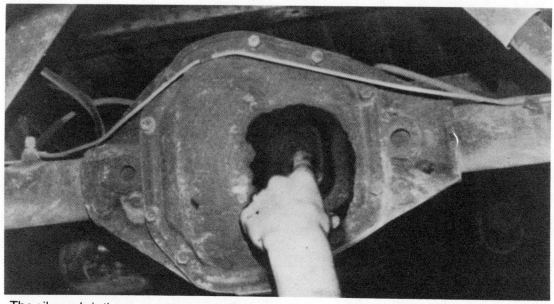

The oil supply in the rear end is checked by removing the drain plug and sticking a finger in to see if the fluid level is up.

THE STANDARD TRANSMISSION

Although still fairly complex, the standard transmission is much simplier in both form and function than the automatic design. Therefore, the standard transmission doesn't absorb as much of the engine's power and delivers somewhat better economy. You can check the fluid level with a dipstick or through a plug in the side of the transmission case. Remove the plug (usually pictured in the shop manual) and reach your finger inside. The oil should be just below the level of the hole.

The clutch is a fairly simple and rugged mechanism, but it occasionally needs an adjustment. From fully engaged to fully disengaged, it only moves a few thousandths of an inch, but it can wear more than that in 20,000 miles. Adjustment is usually quite simple. See your shop manual.

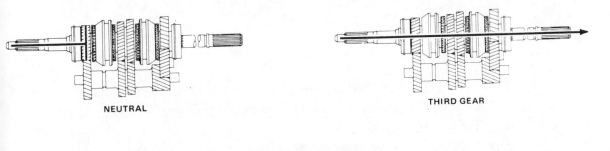

NEUTRAL

THIRD GEAR

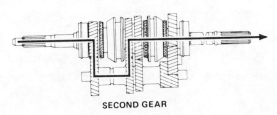

SECOND GEAR

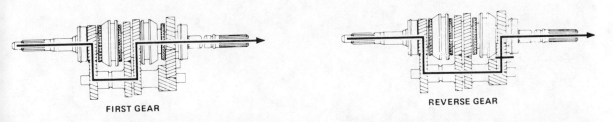

FIRST GEAR

REVERSE GEAR

This illustration shows the gears of a standard transmission and how engine drive is transmitted through the different gears.

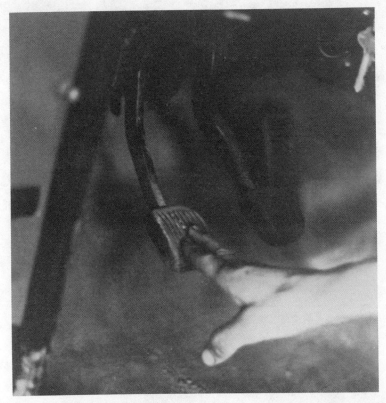

The clutch pedal in standard-transmission-equipped cars should be depressed about one-to-two inches, before resistance is felt. If the pedal goes down too far before the clutch disengages, the clutch is either worn or badly out of adjustment.

Check out the driveshaft for wear in the U-joints. With the car elevated, grasp the driveshaft with both hands and twist it in a rotational manner. There should be very little play in the U-joints.

Sometimes the U-joints may stick from lack of lubrication. See if there are any grease fittings on them so that you may lube them. Replacing U-joints isn't beyond the skills of an amateur.

Don't forget to check the differential's oil supply which has a plug in the side very much like the transmission's. Checking is done in the same way.

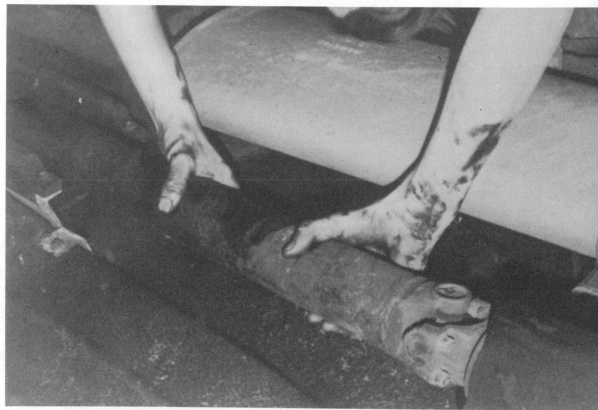

Twisting the driveshaft will reveal whether there's any excess wear in the U-joints. There should be very little movement when the shaft is twisted back and forth.

THE EXHAUST SYSTEM

While you're under the car, take a look at your exhaust pipe.

Aside from leaks where they join together, the exhaust pipe and muffler are most vulnerable to rust. Considering their proximity to the road, these components are constantly splashed by water during rain. In winter, it's worse yet, as the salt used to melt snow and ice accelerates the rusting problem.

Because the exhaust pipe and muffler are so vulnerable to rust, you should make it a point to check them every so often. Even small leaks can allow exhaust gases to find their way into the passenger area.

The muffler is that oval-shaped cannister that attaches to the exhaust pipe and absorbs the exhaust noises. The muffler has a series of tubes or baffles inside of it that modifies the exhaust-gas flow somewhat to make it quieter as it exits into the atmosphere.

Should any part of the exhaust pipe, muffler, or tailpipe suffer damage in the way of a large dent from a rock or something, the flow of exhaust gases can be seriously reduced. There are usually flexible straps supporting the exhaust system as it must be free to float with the car's movement.

In addition to the noises it can emit, any part of the exhaust system that is in contact with the underside of the car poses a possible fire hazard.

The problem of heat becomes even more serious with the advent of the catalytic converter on many new cars. This device is similar to a conventional muffler, but it incorporates a special filtering element that removes exhaust pollutants before the exhaust gas enters the atmosphere. A drawback to the catalytic converter is that it does generate considerable heat. There have been instances where it has resulted in a car's undercoating catching fire.

If your new car has a converter, you must burn only unleaded gas in it, or else the filtering element will become contaminated from the lead in regular gas.

Late model cars have some devices that lower the amount of pollutant in the exhaust gases.

One such emissions control is known as an Air Injection Reacter or AIR. It functions by having a belt-driven pump inject fresh air into tubes located on the exhaust manifold, where the exhaust gases exit from the combustion chambers. As the exhaust gases pass around the open exhaust valve, a stream of air is injected into the exhaust gases, causing them to reburn at very high temperatures. In this way, unburned hydrocarbons get ignited before they can enter (and pollute) the atmosphere.

A check valve is included in the AIR system to preclude exhaust gases from flowing back to the pump and impairing it.

Another part of the AIR system is the anti-backfire valve. Whenever the driver's foot releases the gas pedal, a rich mixture of air and gas finds its way into the combustion chambers. This rich mixture doesn't burn too well and much of it ends up in the exhaust manifold, or even the exhaust pipe.

If the rich mixture should combine with the fresh air entering the exhaust manifold from the air pump, an explosion could take place.

So the anit-backfire valve, operating only momentarily, shuts off that flow of fresh air until the extra-rich mixture passes on through. The air that enters the AIR pump is filtered by either a small filter located on the pump or by the air filter located on the carburetor.

Check you owner's manual to see if the air pump for your car requires any lubrication. And check the driving belt for glazing, cracks, and wear.

The Exhaust Gas Recirculation (EGR) system is yet another device that modern cars incorporate to lower exhaust pollutants. Here a certain portion of the exhaust gases is rerouted back through the carburetor for additional burning.

When emissions controls start acting up, your best bet is to take the car back to the dealer or to the local garage for servicing. Operating with faulty emissions controls will rob your car of good gas mileage. If tune-ups are important for older cars, you can imagine how critical they are for new cars that are laden with all kinds of pollution-fighting devices.

Emissions controls do make engines run erratically and deliver less economy than many of the engines in the past. But automotive technology is coping with the problems. And Mother Nature must have her air supply protected, even if it means putting up with some inconvenience now in the way our cars operate. But you can bet that someday there'll be cleaner-operating, better-running cars for us to drive.

And, once more, carbon monoxide is deadly. Play it safe and replace any component that leaks.

Chapter 16

YOUR STEERING AND SUSPENSION

The steering and suspension systems play vital roles, too, in doubling your car's performance. You want your set of wheels to respond precisely to your touch on the wheel. What's more, if the suspension can't keep the tires on the road, even good steering isn't going to mean that much.

HOW YOUR CAR STEERS

The motion you impart to the steering wheel is transferred to the front wheels in a rather devious manner. First, that wheel in your hands is on a shaft that has on its other end the steering gearbox. This gearbox changes rotary motion (turning the wheel) to a side-to-side motion. Different models do it in different ways. Consult your shop manual to see exactly how it operates. Note the lubrication points and also where the adjustment for the "play" in the steering is located. It is somewhere on the steering gearbox. This is usually a large set screw with a lock nut on it. If you have more than a few inches of free play at the steering wheel, it is a very simple adjustment to make. The rods that go from this box to the wheels usually have some kind of ball and socket connectors on the ends which should move, but not loosely. Other ball joints (larger) hold the wheel and brake assembly to the control arm or arms that are attached at the other ends to the frame. All of this is designed to let the wheels bounce through holes as you steer them in whatever direction you choose while holding up their end of a three or four thousand pound car. It's hard work and wearing.

Ball-joint wear can be minimized by keeping the front end properly greased. Along with grease fittings on the ball joints, you'll find other fittings on suspension joints, steering linkage, etc. The advantage of having your own grease gun is not so much the few dollars you'll save by not taking it to a service station; it's the fact that you'll do a more thorough job, probably, and not miss any vital fittings.

With the front end jacked up, grasp the tire at the top and bottom and shake it back and forth. Worn wheel bearings will result in the wheel wiggling and possibly making a clunking noise. Worn ball joints can also manifest themselves in this manner.

Some idea of wear in the ball joints can be had by grasping front wheel and rocking it vigorously back and forth.

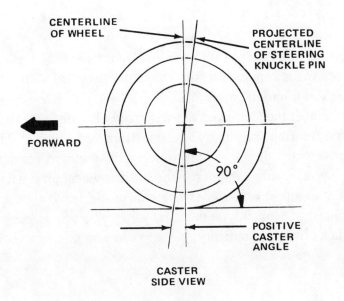

CENTERLINE
OF WHEEL

PROJECTED
CENTERLINE
OF STEERING
KNUCKLE PIN

FORWARD

90°

POSITIVE
CASTER
ANGLE

CASTER
SIDE VIEW

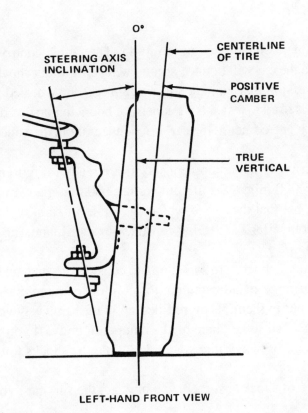

0°

STEERING AXIS
INCLINATION

CENTERLINE
OF TIRE

POSITIVE
CAMBER

TRUE
VERTICAL

LEFT-HAND FRONT VIEW

These two drawings depict two important dimensions that have a vital effect on the way your car steers. The top illustration shows the caster angle, which is the distance the tire's contact patch trails behind the wheel's steering axis; the lower drawing shows camber, which is the angle the tire's centerline makes with the wheel's steering axis.

POWER STEERING

Power-steering maintenance isn't too involved. Check the fluid reservoir level. Before you unscrew the cap and dipstick, wipe the cover off with a cloth to remove any dirt that could fall into the reservoir.

Do you remember the section on tire-wear patterns in the chapter on tires? If you notice your tires wearing irregularly, get the front end aligned. The more rough surfaces you drive over, the more your front end is going to get out of alignment. When driving, if you feel any vibration in the steering wheel, or if it moves from side-to-side in a "shimmying" fashion, the wheels are probably out of balance. If they are, have them balanced dynamically at the local garage. Some garages use a "bubble" balancer to balance wheels statically, but it's still not as effective as the dynamic method.

SHOCK ABSORBERS

These components have a tough job to do. They must control the suspension's movements or else the car will bounce around wildly. Without shocks your car would give you the impression that you are still sitting in a four-wheeled pogostick.

Some methods used to test shocks consist of bouncing up and down on bumpers, or pushing down on one corner of the car. If it bounces more than once, you need a new shock.

As a rule, most original-equipment shocks are ready for retirement after they've gone 10,000 to 15,000 miles. So, if your car has had that many miles or more on its shocks, it's a safe bet that they need replacing. On most cars, replacing shocks isn't beyond the do-it-yourselfer's skills, but consult your shop manual again to be sure your car is one of them.

Rear-mounted air shocks are something to consider if you haul heavy loads. You can obtain a wide range of adjustments for comfort or handling by regulating the amount of air you put in them. They're filled up in the same way you'd inflate a tire. The air-valve is attached somewhere on the bumper or body. If you're going to haul a trailer or a trunk load of heavy items, simply inflate the shocks to the recommended pressure.

Whatever type of shock absorbers you buy, get the very best you can. Stay away

126

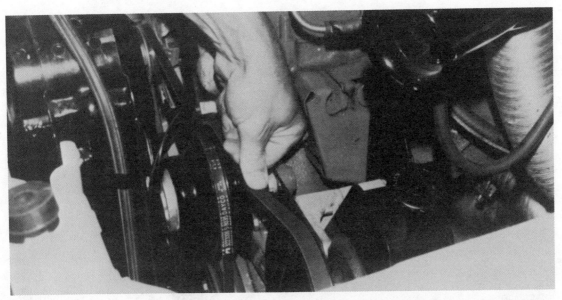

For the power-steering unit to work effectively, the drive belt that operates the pump must be tensioned properly. It should have about ½ to ¾-inch of slack when depressed with your thumb.

Handling can be improved by the addition of traction bars on the rear springs. However, the improvement in handling is made at the expense of riding comfort.

from the "cheapie" bargains; they won't last as long as a good brand. Worse, they won't provide very good damping while they are in service.

As you can imagine from this chapter and other chapters, you can spend a fair amount of time underneath your car just checking things out.

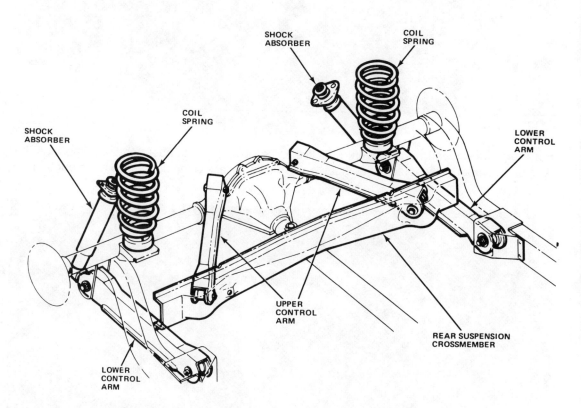

Here is a drawing of the rear coil-suspension setup on some cars.

IMPORTANT INSTALLATION INFORMATION

FRONT UNITS

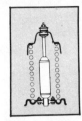

Shock Absorbers and Stabilizing Units are usually installed in the same position and in the same manner as those originally used on the car.

If units are to be otherwise installed, special instructions will be supplied with the unit.

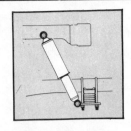

REAR UNITS

IMPORTANT: In some cases, when installing shock absorbers or Front Stabilizing Units it may be necessary to slightly enlarge the hole in the lower suspension arm to permit the unit to pass thru. This can be done by tapping the inside edge of the hole or by filing or grinding. Enlarge hole just enough to allow unit to pass thru.
CAUTION: Do not file or grind the unit.

IMPORTANT: When installing shock absorbers or Rear Stabilizing Units, make sure that hydraulic brake lines, gas lines and tail pipes are clear of the units. All clearances must be checked with the car body both up and down (with wheels hanging and the body pushed down). When necessary move all lines and tail pipes to obtain clearance.

SHOULDERED STEM

TIGHTEN NUT UNTIL RETAINER BOTTOMS ON STEM SHOULDER.

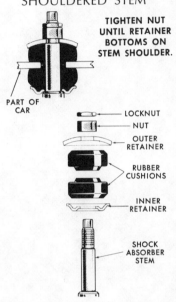

PART OF CAR

LOCKNUT
NUT
OUTER RETAINER
RUBBER CUSHIONS
INNER RETAINER
SHOCK ABSORBER STEM

NON-SHOULDERED STEM

TIGHTEN NUT UNTIL CUSHIONS BULGE ALMOST TO OUTER EDGE OF RETAINERS. DO NOT TIGHTEN EXCESSIVELY.

PART OF CAR

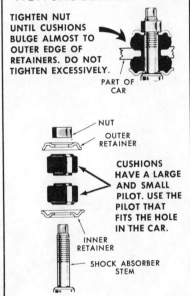

NUT
OUTER RETAINER

CUSHIONS HAVE A LARGE AND SMALL PILOT. USE THE PILOT THAT FITS THE HOLE IN THE CAR.

INNER RETAINER
SHOCK ABSORBER STEM

CROSS PIN MOUNTING

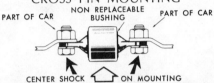

PART OF CAR — NON REPLACEABLE BUSHING — PART OF CAR

CENTER SHOCK ON MOUNTING

FLATTENED ENDS OF X-PIN ARE PRE-SET TO FIT SQUARE AGAINST MOUNTING PLATE AT NORMAL CAR HEIGHT. WHEN INSTALLING, IF FLATS ARE NOT SQUARE WITH PLATE — ROTATE SHOCK HALF TURN FOR BETTER ALIGNMENT.

USE NEW MOUNTING PIN PARTS TO REPLACE THE ORIGINAL PIN

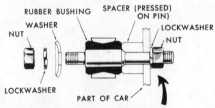

RUBBER BUSHING   SPACER (PRESSED) ON PIN)
WASHER   LOCKWASHER
NUT   NUT
LOCKWASHER   PART OF CAR

BE SURE MOUNTING PIN IS EXTRA TIGHT TO PREVENT IT FROM LOOSENING

MOUNTING WITHOUT INNER SLEEVE

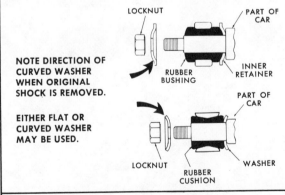

LOCKNUT   PART OF CAR
RUBBER BUSHING
INNER RETAINER

NOTE DIRECTION OF CURVED WASHER WHEN ORIGINAL SHOCK IS REMOVED.

EITHER FLAT OR CURVED WASHER MAY BE USED.

PART OF CAR
LOCKNUT   WASHER
RUBBER CUSHION

MOUNTING WITH INNER SLEEVE

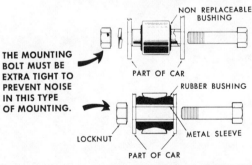

NON REPLACEABLE BUSHING

PART OF CAR

THE MOUNTING BOLT MUST BE EXTRA TIGHT TO PREVENT NOISE IN THIS TYPE OF MOUNTING.

RUBBER BUSHING
LOCKNUT   METAL SLEEVE
PART OF CAR

MAKE SURE METAL SLEEVE IS INSULATED IN RUBBER BUSHING. RE-USE MOUNTING BOLT, NUT AND LOCKWASHER.

DO

1. OBSERVE THE LOCATION of all mounting parts, washers, retainers, etc. as they are removed, and be sure to reassemble these parts in the same positions.

2. USE CARE when installing the new units. Be sure all nuts and bolts are securely tightened. Check clearances.

3. FOLLOW SPECIAL INSTRUCTIONS WHEN SUPPLIED WITH UNITS.

DO NOT

1. DO NOT TWIST OFF STUDS. If nuts are rusted, use penetrating oil on threads, allowing a few minutes for the oil to penetrate before unscrewing. If nut has rusted to a point where penetrating oil does not permit removal, it is recommended that a nut-splitter be used, taking care not to damage the threads on the mounting, if it is part of the car.

2. DO NOT GRIP POLISHED PISTON ROD with tools during installation. This will damage rod and cause unit failure.

3. DO NOT HANG WHEELS on cars having rear coil springs or air springs when changing shock absorbers.

(Courtesy Monroe)

Chapter 17

PERFORMANCE DRIVING

We've now come to the most important element in "doubling your car's performance"—YOU!

Regardless of what you've done to your car to put it into top running condition, you're the one who will determine how well that mechanical complex is going to perform where it counts: on the road.

If you've undertaken some of the maintenance tasks described in this book, you should have a deeper understanding of your car. By being intimate with your piece of machinery, you are sure to gain a certain respect or reverence for it. You are able to see your car as an assemblage of various parts, each of which has something important to contribute to the total machine.

After you've made that final adjustment and put away your tools, you're now ready to reap the fruits of your labor.

So, climb in behind the wheel and get ready to head for the open road. You're ready for performance driving.

The first thing you want to do when you slide behind the wheel is to get positioned properly. An ideal seat cushion should slope slightly down toward the seat back, curve slightly up on the sides to cradle your thighs and be long enough to support your legs out to the backs of your knees.

The ideal seat back should have a little wrap around your hips and sides and have an angle that will let you lean back, completely relaxed, and still be looking straight ahead at the pavement. Now, this terrific seat should be foreward enough to have the seat brace you when you push hard on the brakes, but still back far enough to be able to turn the wheel hard without banging your elbows into your ribs or the door. That ideal place might be hard to find, but you can come close to it using whatever seat adjustments you have or even a cushion or two. The idea is to take a comfortable, relaxed position behind the wheel and become ONE with your car.

Few drivers ever give any thought to the manner in which they operate their pedals. Smooth, progressive motion on all the pedals is desirable for three reasons: fuel economy, durability and comfort. One quick and simple way to develop this motion is to try to rest your heels on the floor at all times and push the pedals, for the most part, with your toes and the ball of your foot as though you were trying to feel something with your toes. You can pivot your foot from gas to brake pedal quicker and more accurately if you don't have to lift your leg. Keeping the left heel on the floor while operating the clutch eliminates the lurching starts traditional with manual-shifting beginners. It also saves the clutch, gear, U-joints and composure. Developing a smooth, ''feather touch'' on the accelerator can increase your miles-per-gallon figure dramatically and make your car more responsive.

When you accelerate, particularly from a dead stop, don't stamp on the pedal: instead, use a smooth, progressive action.

The same goes when you're operating the brakes: use a smooth, progressive pressure on the brake pedal. Don't wait until you're almost on top of something before you decide to ''throw out the anchor.''

Last-instant deceleration builds up heat in the linings or pads, making them wear faster.

Learn how to really use the brakes. For instance, you know that the brakes must be operated in a ''pumping'' fashion to prevent skids on wet roads. And, you brake before a turn; not while you're going through it.

If your car is equipped with a standard transmission, you have yet another control in the clutch for which you must develop a smooth touch.

Even just starting up the engine involves a certain amount of consideration and technique. When you first start up an engine that has been shut off for awhile, don't rev it up wildly. Give it a few seconds or so to allow the oil to circulate, before you increase the rpm. If the engine has been exposed to the cold, as during overnight, give it a couple of minutes of warm-up before you start out.

As soon as an engine is turned off, oil starts draining off the cylinder walls and other bearing surfaces. So, if you start it up later and immediately take off, the oil

132

hasn't had a chance to form a protective film between the bearing surfaces. That's the reason most engine wear can occur when an engine has just been started.

Don't, however, allow an engine to idle fast for long with the automatic choke closed. What happens with the choke closed is that the engine is getting a higher ratio of gas to air, and that will tend to dilute the oil film on the cylinder walls. Here again, more wear will result when the piston and cylinder walls make contact. After the engine has idled for a few moments, tap the gas pedal sharply to open the choke and normalize the gas/air mixture.

Instead of having a prolonged warm-up, give the oil a chance to circulate, and take off, gradually increasing the car's speed. If you start off rather slowly, and progressively build up the vehicle's motion to normal cruising speed, you give the oil a chance to thin and spread its protective film.

Even if the engine has had a prolonged warm-up by idling it during cold weather, you still should start off moderately slow, because the lubricant in the transmission, wheel bearings, and rear end hasn't had any exposure to heat. It will need to warm up to operating temperature gradually, too.

Driving is a science that encompasses all kinds of situations. Besides striving to develop smooth, positive control movement, you must learn how to relate to road conditions.

READ THE ROAD

Besides keeping your car equipped with good tires, you must also learn how to evaluate a wide variety of surface conditions to determine their tractional properties.

On dry roads, you don't have to worry too much about traction. But even on them, there can be deposits of sand, stones, oil accumulation, and damp spots underneath over-hanging trees, that can turn an otherwise safe road into a skid-hazard.

Don't take for granted that just because a road looks dry, your tires won't have any trouble maintaining traction. If you study that seemingly dry and stable surface, you just might find a sprinkling of sand or stones (or some other substance) that may induce a skid. And, if it's a sharp turn, entertain the possibility that your car could skid over onto the other side of the road and collide with an oncoming vehicle.

Your chances for skidding on a wet road are obviously greater than on a dry

z

133

surface. But aside from the skid hazard, wet roads present another dangerous phenomenon: hydroplaning.

During a skid the tires are still in contact with the road; but if hydroplaning occurs, the tires (usually the front ones) actually plane, or "ski" on a wedge of water. Naturally, with your front tires planing, your speed control is gone.

There are several factors that contribute to hydroplaning: condition and size of the tires, speed and the amount of water on the road.

If the tires are worn, water gets trapped underneath them, because there's little or no grooving in the tread to channel away the water from underneath the tires. In addition, if the tires are quite wide, there's more surface area with which to plane.

The faster the vehicle is traveling, moreover, the more easily the tires will "lift."

Finally, there has to be enough water present. How much? A rule-of-thumb estimate is that if there's enough water on the road for falling raindrops to produce a "dimpling" effect, your car could turn into an automotive surfboard. File the above statements somewhere in the back of your mind; then recall them the next time you get ready to travel on a wet road.

Whether roads are wet or dry, get into the habit of really studying them.

By paying attention to surface conditions, you'll notice features about them that would normally escape your awareness.

THE OTHER GUY

Along with reading the road, you should also learn how to read the other guy behind the wheel.

In other words, become a student of human nature; study the actions of other drivers. Also, assume that they don't see you. In that way you'll drive more defensively. Drive as though you are invisible.

Because you always have to be on the lookout for the other guy, get into the habit of looking over both shoulders before you switch lanes or pull away from curbs and parking areas. Don't rely on mirrors to reveal the presence of any vehicles behind you. Mirrors have blind spots. You may think it somewhat uncomfortable at first to turn your head to the sides frequently to keep tabs on traffic behind—and beside—you; but it's not as uncomfortable as colliding with someone you didn't see.

Vow to yourself that you're going to become a better driver and to learn more about your car. Hopefully, this book will help you.

The next time you slide behind the wheel, take a moment before you start out, and think how much your car does for you. It's a pretty marvelous piece of machinery, isn't it? Happy motoring!

Part IV

GLOSSARY

A

ATF: Automatic transmission fluid.

Accelerator pump: The plunger-like mechanism of the carburetor that squirts extra gas into the throat, or air intake, when the gas pedal is depressed.

Air cleaner: The filter element that sits on top of the carburetor and traps dirt particles so that they can't enter the engine and create wear.

Air/fuel ratio: The amount of air mixed with a certain amount of gasoline. The ratio of air to gas that provided optimum power is about 15:1; that is, 15-parts of air to one part of gas.

Air-injection system: Part of the emissions-controls setup on modern cars. It functions by injecting fresh air into the exhaust manifold and by causing the exhaust gases to burn at extremely high temperatures, thereby reducing the number of unburned hydrocarbons that exit into the atmosphere.

Air intake: The inlet in the air-filter, carburetor and ventilation system where fresh air enters.

Air pump: That part of the air-injection system that pumps air into the exhaust manifold.

Air shock: A type of shock absorber used on the rear suspension and filled with air to increase the vehicle's load-carrying capacity.

Alligator clip: A temporary fastener, so named because it looks like an alligator's jaw. Used for securing wire when performing tests.

Alternator: The electricity-producing component of the engine that is driven mechanically by a belt. Replaces the generator on most modern cars.

Ammeter: An instrument for measuring the current flow in the electrical system. When mounted on the instrument panel, it shows whether the charging system is functioning or not.

Amp: Abbreviation for ampere. It is a unit of measurement for the flow of electrical current.

Anti-backfire valve: The device in the air-injection system that prevents backfiring from occurring in the exhaust manifold.

Anti-freeze: A substance like ethylene glycol, which is added to the water in the radiator to prevent the cooling system from freezing or boiling over.

Anti-stall dashpot: Device on the carburetor that allows the throttle linkage to return slowly when the gas pedal is released to cut emissions.

Armature: The rotating member of a motor, like a starter or generator.

Asbestos: Material used in clutch and brake linings where resistance to extreme heating is required.

Automatic choke: The setup on most modern carburetors in which the choke valve is operated thermostatically.

Automatic transmission: A transmission that uses a varying hydraulic pressure to change gears.

Axle: The crosswise member of the car that supports the wheels. It may be a one-piece unit or articulated, so that the wheels can move independently of each other.

Axle bearings: (Rear) situated near the outer ends of the axle, they support it and permit it to turn easily. (Front) inside the brake drum or disc.

140

B

BTDC: Before top dead center. This term applies to the distance a piston is from the top of its stroke, as it moves up the bore of the cylinder.

Ball joint: A ball/socket that's part of the linkage setup that connects the front wheel to the control arms of the front suspension.

Ballast resistor: A device such as a high-resistance wire that lowers battery voltage going to the point assembly in the distributor, so that the points don't burn from excessive voltage.

Battery: The box-like structure that generates electricity by the electrochemical process between the electrolyte and plates when the battery is put into circuit.

Battery hydrometer: An instrument consisting of a glass tube with a hollow rubber ball on one end that is used to test the specific gravity or "strength" of the electrolyte.

Bead: The inner-circumference part of a tire that holds it onto the wheel.

Bellhousing: The half-rounded structure that houses the main components of the clutch, like the disc, pressure plate, and throwout fork.

Belt: Common term for any of the driveline belts that drive the alternator, power steering pump, air pump, water pump, etc. Also applies to the layer of material that encircles a tire's plies.

Bendix drive: That part of the starter mechanism that engages the starter gear with the flywheel to turn the engine over when the key is turned on.

BHP: Brake horsepower. Horsepower.

Bias-belted: A tire design in which layers or "belts" of material like fiberglass or steel encircle the plies around the circumference of the tire.

141

Bias ply: A conventional tire in which there are no belts, just two or more plies with their cords placed at angles to the beads.

Bleeder valve: Small valve behind the wheel that is cracked open to ''bleed'' the brake lines of air pockets.

Brake: Mechanism that retards the rotational movement of the wheel.

Brake-backing plate: Part of the brake assembly to which the brake shoes are attached.

Brake energization: Self-adjusting characteristic of modern brakes.

Brake fluid: The special fluid that is put into the brake master cylinders to activate the wheel cylinders located in the wheel/brake assembly.

Brake lines: The metal and rubber lines that run from the master cylinder to the wheels' backing plates.

Brake linings: The frictional materials that bear against the drum or disc to stop the wheel.

Brake shoes: Curved components on which the linings are bonded or riveted.

Breaker plate: Circular disc or plate in the distrbutor on which the breaker points are located.

Breaker points: Known commonly as the points; they produce the sparks at the sparkplugs by opening at a precise time when a cam mechanism pushes them apart.

Brush: A small piece of carbon in generators and alternators that picks up current produced by these components and transfers it elsewhere.

Bushing: Tubular or washer-shaped material that serves as a bearing.

Butterfly valve: Circular piece of metal that pivots on a shaft and that closes off or opens up an area such as the carburetor bore or throat.

C

Cable clamp: Attaches the battery cable to the battery post.

Caliper: C-shaped component that fits over the edge of the brake disc containing a slave cylinder and pressure pads.

Cam: A shaft with an eccentric cross section. A good example is the breaker cam in the distributor: it opens the points when a spark plug must fire.

Camshaft: The long shaft inside the engine that operates the valves directly (overhead cam engine) or operates the valves through rocker arms and pushrods (overhead or side valve engine) to open and close the valves in the cylinder head.

Capacitor: Small tubular device that stores electrical current. More commonly known as a condenser in conventional ignition systems.

Carbon: Sooty material formed as a byproduct of the combustion process in an engine.

Carbon monoxide: Toxic gas that is colorless, odorless, and tasteless. Also formed by combustion.

Carburetor: The component that mixes the air and gasoline in the right proportions before introducing it into the combustion chambers.

Caster: The slant from verticle of the front axle's pivot points that give a front tire the tendency to track straight ahead.

Catalytic converter: Small muffler-like device that contains special filtering element for absorbing harmful hydrocarbons from the exhaust gases before they can enter the atmosphere.

143

Cell: One of the compartments of a battery. A six-volt battery has three cells; a twelve-volt battery has six cells.

Centrifugal advance: The springs and weights in the distributor that rotates the breaker plate when the engine is revved up from the idle-speed setting for the purpose of advancing the ignition timing.

Charcoal canister: Cylindrical container containing charcoal filtering element that absorbs fumes from the gas tank and introduces them into the engine where they are burned.

Charging system: Wires and components that keep the battery charged. The alternator or generator has the major task of keeping the battery charge.

Choke: The part of the carburetor that restricts the intake of fresh air into the carburetor for the purpose of making a cold engine easier to start.

Choke plate: See Butterfly valve.

Circuit breaker: Functions like a fuse; automatically breaks a circuit when the flow of current becomes too high for the safe-load carrying capacity of a wire. It's resettable, unlike a fuse, which must be replaced when it blows.

Clutch: Used in standard transmissions; couples engine power to the drive shaft.

Clutch disc: Located between the flywheel of the engine and the pressure plate of the clutch assembly. Its high-friction surfaces provide the means by which the engine's power links up with the rear drive train.

CO: Chemical abbreviation for carbon monoxide.

Coil: Member of the ignition system that converts low-voltage current into high voltage necessary to fire the spark plugs.

Combustion chamber: Upper part of the cylinder in which the burning occurs.

144

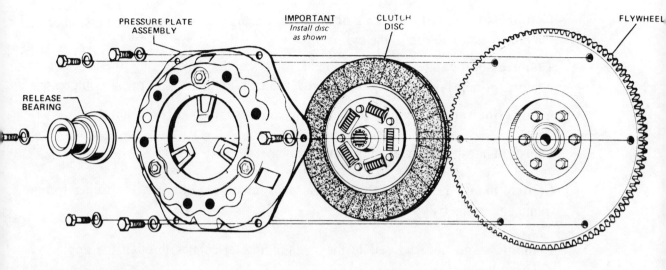

PRESSURE PLATE
ASSEMBLY

IMPORTANT
*Install disc
as shown*

CLUTCH
DISC

FLYWHEEL

RELEASE
BEARING

(Cutaway of a clutch)

The Charging System

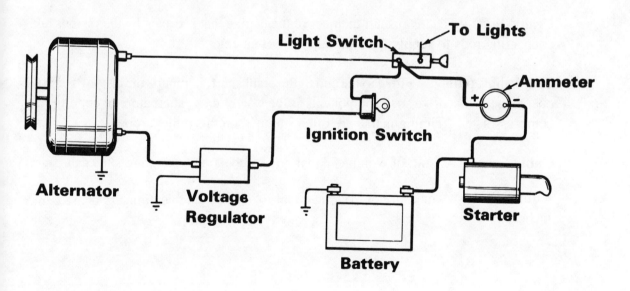

Light Switch

To Lights

Ammeter

Ignition Switch

Alternator

Voltage
Regulator

Battery

Starter

Compression: The squeezing of the air/gas charge in the combustion chamber by the piston as it rises up in the cylinder.

Compression gauge: An instrument for accurately measuring the amount of compression (in pounds,) that is produced inside the cylinder as the piston compresses.

Connecting rod: Component that "connects" the piston to the crankshaft.

Constant-mesh gears: Gears that are always meshed together.

Control arm: Located in the front suspension system of a car, it attaches to the frame and to the ball joints.

Coolant: The fluid housed in the radiator that circulates through the engine to dissipate heat.

Cooling system: Comprised of the radiator, water pump, water jackets, radiator cap, thermostat, fan, hoses, and drive belts.

Cotter key: Bobby-pin shaped piece of wire that fits through a hole in a shaft or rod to secure some component on it.

Crankcase: The lower housing of the engine that contains the crankshaft.

Crankshaft: The main shaft member of the engine that is driven by the pistons and connecting rods to supply the motive power of an engine.

Crankshaft pulley: Fitted to the end of the crankshaft, it imparts the driving force to operate belts that drive such components as the water pump, alternator, air conditioner compressor, etc. Timing marks are often stamped on this pulley, too.

Cubic inch: A unit of volume equal to a cube one inch long on each side.

Cubic Litre: A measure of volume equal to 1,000 cubic centimeters or 61 cubic inches.

Curb idle screw: The screw on the carburetor that regulates the speed at which the engine idles when no pressure is exerted on the gas pedal.

Cutout: An automatic switch that prevents the battery from discharging through the generator.

Cylinder: That part of the engine that houses the piston and valves.

Cylinder block: The part of the engine that houses all the cylinders.

Cylinder head: The portion of the engine that sits on top of the cylinder block and that houses the valves and combustion chambers.

D

Dashpot: Electrically operated device that automatically closes the throttle valve in the carburetor all the way to prevent the engine from continuing to run on when the ignition is turned off.

Detonation: Commonly known as "knock", it results when the air/gas mixture burns unevenly. See Pre-ignition.

Dieseling: Occurs when the engine continues to run on after the ignition has been shut off.

Differential: The ring/pinion and spider gears in the drive axle.

Diode: Small electrical "valve" located in the alternator. Its purpose is to convert the alternating current produced by the alternator into direct current for the electrical system.

Dipstick: A long, thin rod for measuring the oil level.

Disc (brake):   Also known as rotor. The circular piece of metal attached to a wheel against which small pads are pressed when the brake pedal is applied.

Displacement: The volume of a cylinder. The displacement of an engine is measured by taking the volume of one cylinder and multiplying by the number of cylinders.

Distributor: That part of the ignition system that contains the points/condenser. Called a distributor because it ''distributes'' or sends electricity to the spark plugs.

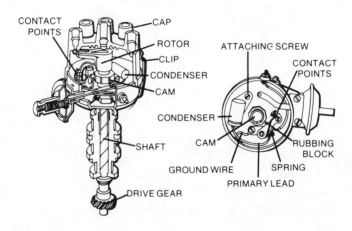

Distributor in a conventional ignition system. (Courtesy Autolite)

Distributor cap: The circular cap of the distributor that contains the ends of the spark plug wires.

D.O.T.:   Department of Transportation. A federal department that determines minimum acceptable standards for vehicle performance.

Drive belt: A term for any belt that drives components like the water pump, air conditioner, etc.

148

Drive line: All the components involved in transferring engine power back to the rear wheels.

Drive shaft: The long shaft underneath the car that transfers power from the transmission to the differential in the rear axle.

Drum (brake):   Attached to the wheel, it provides a braking effect when the brake shoes expand outward and contact the drum with their linings.

Dual throat: A carburetor that has two throats or bores.

Dual exhausts: A split exhaust system to provide minimum back pressure and increase the engine's power.

Dust cap: A cover which keeps moisture and dirt out and keeps dirt in.

Dwell: The number of degrees of breaker-cam travel that the points stay closed in the distributor. Also known as cam angle.

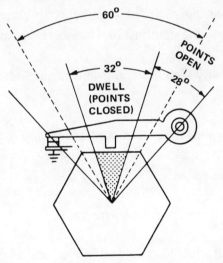

This illustration shows what is meant by dwell, which is the number of degrees that the points remain closed in the distributor.

Dwellmeter: Instrument that measures the amount of dwell in degrees with the engine running.

E

EGR: Abbreviation for exhaust gas recirculation. One of a modern car's emissions controls that functions by reburning a certain portion of its exhaust gases.

Electrical system: Comprises the lighting, starting, charging, and ignition systems.

Electrodes: The two points on a spark plug between which the spark jumps, setting fire to the air/fuel mixture in the combustion chambers.

Electrolyte: The fluid contained in the battery's cells. It's a mixture of water and sulfuric acid.

Electronic ignition: Form of ignition in which transitors replace breaker points and condenser.

Emission controls: Any component on an engine that reduces the pollutants that the engine produces by filtering them before they can enter the atmosphere, or by channeling them back into the combustion chambers where they are burned.

Engine speed: Speed at which the crankshaft turns. Measured in rpm: revolutions per minute.

Equalizer switch: Proportions the amount of braking force between the front and rear brakes so that the rear brakes don't take hold as sharply as the front brakes and cause the rear wheels to lock up.

Ethylene glycol: Specific term for anti-freeze.

Exhaust manifold: Attached to the side of the engine where the exhaust gasses exit from the cylinders, it carries the gases back to the exhaust pipe.

Exhaust pipe: The long pipe that connects between the exhaust manifold and the muffler.

150

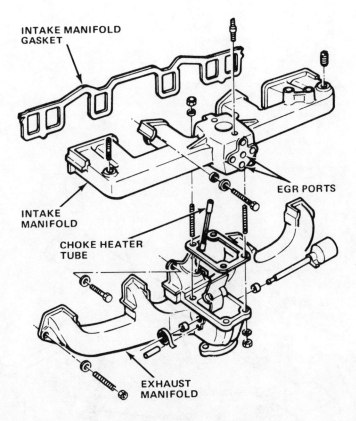

INTAKE MANIFOLD
GASKET

EGR PORTS

INTAKE
MANIFOLD

CHOKE HEATER
TUBE

EXHAUST
MANIFOLD

Here you see what the exhaust manifold looks like, and how it's placed adjacent to the intake manifold for the purpose of heating part of the intake manifold.

Exhaust stroke: The final stroke in the engine's cycle when the exhaust valve opens to let the spent charge out of the combustion chamber, as the piston starts to come back up the cylinder.

Exhaust system: Comprises the exhaust manifold, exhaust pipe, muffler, resonator or catalytic converter, and tail pipe.

Exhaust valve: One of the two valves that are situated in each cylinder.

151

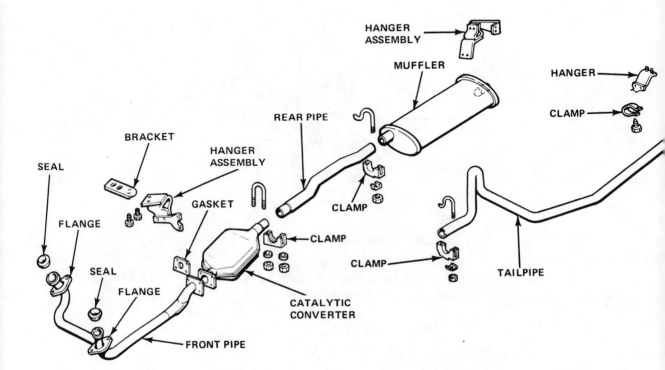

Exhaust System—V-8 with Single Converter

Exploded illustration of an exhaust system showing the front pipes, which attach to the exhaust manifold and the rest of the system's components that are underneath the car. This particular exhaust system shows what a catalytic converter looks like and how it's included in the system of a modern car.

Fan: Located behind the radiator, it is driven by a belt that runs off the crankshaft pulley. The fan assists in cooling the engine at lower speeds by drawing air in through the radiator.

Fast-idle cam: A snail-shaped plate on the side of the carburetor that is held in a certain position by a screw. The fast-idle cam is connected to the choke plate by a choke rod. It raises the idle speed when the engine is cold.

The fast-idle cam is held in position by a screw that rests against one of the "steps" in the snail-shaped cam. Check manufacturer's specs for your particular car, before you attempt to adjust cam setting.

Feeler gauge: A piece of metal of a precise thickness used for measuring gaps.

Fenderwell: The underside of a fender.

Firewall: The partition that separates the engine compartment from the passenger compartment.

Firing order: The order in which the spark plugs fire.

Flexible hanger: Exhaust system supports.

Float: Hollow component inside the carburetor's float bowl that controls the needle valve.

Float chamber: Housing for the float/needle valve assembly.

Float level: The level of the gas that is contained in the float chamber.

Flooding: Condition in which too much gas enters the carburetor and causes an over-rich mixture, which makes the engine hard to start.

Flywheel: The large circular steel disc attached to the crankshaft. The purpose of the flywheel is to smooth out the engine's power pulses.

Four-stroke engine: Describes the modern automobile engine's functions: intake of the air/gas charge; compression of it by the piston; power stroke caused by the spark plugs igniting the charge; and finally, the exhaust stroke where the spent charge or gases exit out the cylinder. Each time the piston moves up or down in its cylinder, it's called a stroke.

Free play: The term that describes the distance a control lever will move before it actuates the mechanism.

Freeze plug: Also called an expansion plug, it's a small circular piece of metal that is pressed into the block of the engine. Its purpose is to give way, should the engine coolant freeze up, and prevent the engine from cracking.

Fuel line: A pipe that transfers gas from the tank to the fuel pump and to the carburetor.

Fuel pump: Delivers gas to the carburetor from the gas tank.

Fuse: A small cylindrical glass housing with metal tips and a strip of low-melting-point metal inside that melts when too much current passes through.

154

Fusible link: A section of wire that functions like a fuse by melting when too much current attempts to pass along the wire.

Fuse panel: A panel or compartment where all the fuses are kept together. Usually located under the instrument panel or on the firewall.

G

Gap: The small distance that separates the electrodes on a spark plug or the points in the breaker-point assembly in the distributor.

Gasket: A layer of material like cork or metal that acts as a seal between two metal surfaces to keep them from leaking air or some other fluid.

Gear: A toothed wheel.

Gear Ratio: Expressed as a numerical ratio, it's the number of revolutions one gear makes in relation to the gear it's meshed with. For example, a ratio of 3:1 means that the smaller gear makes three revolutions for every revolution of the larger gear.

Gearbox: Another term for transmission.

Generator: An electricity-producing component of the engine's electrical system. The generator has been replaced on most modern cars by the alternator.

Grease fitting: Small rounded fitting with a hole in the center for accepting grease and minimizing friction between two components. Ball joints and other members of the front suspension incorporate grease fittings.

Ground: An expression for denoting a wire or electrical component being attached, or "grounded", to some metal part of the car for making a complete circuit in the electrical system.

155

H

Header pipe: A term for exhaust manifold.

HC: Chemical abbreviation for hydrocarbons.

Heater hose: Section of hose that carries coolant from the engine to the heater core.

Heat riser valve: Another term for manifold heat control valve. The purpose is to direct a certain amount of exhaust gas against the intake manifold to help a cold engine warm up more quickly.

This is what a heat riser looks like. The valve in the center is controlled by the heat-sensitive spring and counterweight assembly on the outside.

Heat range: A property of spark plugs. It's a term that denotes how quickly a spark plug dissipates heat.

Horsepower or HP: A unit of measurement for determining an engine's power. One horsepower (HP) is defined as raising a 33,000 pound weight one foot in one minute.

156

Hydraulic system: The braking system is a good example of how hydraulics are used in an automobile. Fluid is transferred under pressure from the master cylinder through tubes to exert pressure against pistons in the slave cylinders, which in turn force the shoes or pads to press against a drum or disc.

Hydrocarbon: Any substance, like gasoline, that is composed mostly of carbon and hydrogen.

Hydroplaning: A condition of wet-road driving whereby the tire(s) act fully separate from the road surface by a layer or wedge of water.

Hypoid gears: Gears with a curved tooth design. The pinion and ring gear in the differential are examples.

I

Idiot light: A somewhat derogatory term for a warning light mounted on the instrument panel. Such a light will glow red or orange when the oil supply is low or if the engine overheats. Many motorists prefer to have gauges in place of the lights for more accurate indications of an engine's status.

Idle circuit: Series of orifices and passages in the carburetor that admit gas into the carburetor throat at idling speeds. The gas enters below the throttle valve.

Idle screw: A screw mounted on the throttle linkage that controls the rpm at which the engine will idle.

Idler arm: A movable brace or support for the steering linkage.

Ignition system: That part of the electrical system that provides the spark in the combustion chamber to fire the intake charge. Spark plugs, spark plug wires, distributor, coil, battery and ignition switch are the major components in the ignition system.

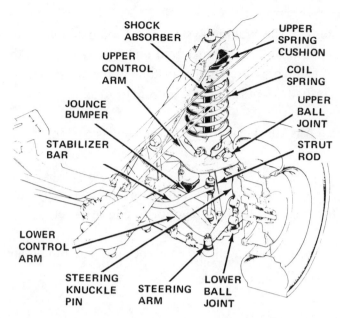

This illustration shows the various components of an independent suspension.

Impeller: The fan-shaped component in the water pump that drives the coolant throughout the engine and radiator.

Independent suspension: A form of suspension in a car whereby each wheel is free to move up and down independently of the other wheels.

Intake charge: Another term for the mixture of air and gas that enters the combustion chamber.

Intake manifold: The part of the engine that the carburetor sits on. It's a series of chambers leading from the carburetor to the various cylinders, for the purpose of directing the charge into the combustion chambers.

Intake valve: Located in the top of the combustion chamber.

I.R.S.: Independent rear suspension. Type of suspension that gives improved ride and control

J

Jet: A small tube with a metered hole in the center of it for atomizing gasoline.

Jumper cables: Two cables with an alligator clamp on each end. Used in hooking up a booster battery to a "dead" battery for giving the latter a temporary charge to start the engine.

K

Kingpin: A part of the front-wheel assembly on older cars. It serves the same purpose as ball joints on modern cars.

Knock: Same as detonation. Occurs when gas and air burn unevenly, or explode in combustion chamber.

L

Late spark: Occurs when ignition timing is retarded. Instead of the spark plug firing when the piston is rising near TDC (top dead center), the piston will have reached TDC and started back down before the spark plug fires.

Lbs. per HP: Pounds per horsepower.

Lead free: Gasoline that doesn't contain lead additives. New cars with catalytic converters require lead-free gas.

Leaf spring: The type of spring used on the rear suspension of many cars. It's a length of flat steel that connects the frame to the axle.

Lean mixture: Too much air to the amount of gas present in the intake charge.

Linkage: A series of rods, levers, and springs.

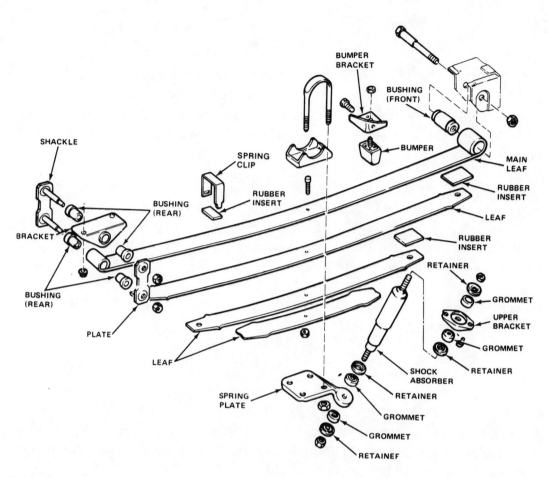

This illustration shows how a leaf spring is constructed. Instead of coil springs, leaf springs are used on some cars.

Lifter: A small, cylindrical component that rides between the camshaft lobe and the pushrod. The lifter is usually of the hydraulic type, which automatically compensates for any play between the cam lobe and the final operation of opening and closing a valve.

Limiter cap: A small plastic cap that fits over the adjustment screws on a modern carburetor to limit the range of movement the screw can be turned, so that the carburetor isn't adjusted beyond its capacity to affect emissions controls.

Limited-slip differential: A type of rear-end differential in which if one wheel starts spinning free, the drive from the engine is automatically directed to the other wheel to effect better traction.

Liner: A sleeve insert that fits into the cylinder hole in the engine block.

Litre: A fluid measure equal to 1.05 quarts.

Lobe: The eccentric, or "egg shaped", cross section of a camshaft that imparts motion to the lifter to cause a valve in the cylinder head to open or close. Conventional ignition systems also have lobes on the distributor shaft to open the points.

Low-tension leads: Wiring in the ignition system that carries low-voltage loads. Consists of battery cables, plus and minus coil-wire connections, and wiring to the distributor and ignition switch.

M

MPG: Miles per gallon.

Main bearings: The bearings that support the crankshaft.

Manual choke: The system whereby the choke plate in the carburetor bore is closed and opened manually by a cable from the driver's position.

Master cylinder: Main reservoir for the brake fluid in the engine compartment.

Misfire: Occurs when spark plugs don't fire when they should, such as would occur if the plug wires from the distributor cap were connected to the wrong spark plugs.

Modulator: Small device on automatic transmission that operates by engine vacuum to make smoother gear shifting.

Motor mounts: The attachments that hold the engine in place.

Muffler: Oval-or cylindrically-formed cannister underneath the car that contains some form of baffling or absorption material to "slow down" the exhaust gases in order to reduce the noise they make.

Multimeter: Instrument that contains the functions of an ammeter, voltmeter, and an ohmmeter, so that multiple tests can be performed.

N

Needle valve: Controls the amount of gas that enters the float bowl of the carburetor by the movement of the float, as it rises or falls according to the level of gas in the bowl.

Neutral safety switch: An electrical safety device contained in the starting/ignition system to prevent the engine from starting when the transmission is in gear.

O

Odometer: Mileage indicator. Part of the speedometer.

OHC: Overhead cam. An engine design in which the shaft that operates the valve gear is located in the top of the engine.

O-ring: A seal that is O-shaped.

Ohm: The term that means resistance in an electrical system.

Oil-control ring: A type of piston ring that controls the amount of oil film on the cylinder wall.

Oil cooler: A radiator for cooling oil.

Oil filter: A metal canister that contains a filtering element for removing dirt and other impurities from the oil.

Oil pan: The main reservoir for the engine oil. Located on the bottom of the engine.

Oil pressure: The amount of pressure measured in pounds per square inch that the oil is under as it flows through the engine.

Oil pump: The component in the engine that pumps the oil through the engine.

Output shaft: The shaft that transfers the drive from the transmission to the driveshaft.

Overdrive: A gear ratio that is higher than 1 to 1.

Overflow tube: A narrow tube that runs from the neck of the radiator filler-opening down alongside the radiator so that excessive coolant can escape.

P

PCV: Positive crankcase valve. A one-way air valve. One of a car's emissions control devices that pipes oil vapors from the crankcase and into the combustion chambers where they are burned, to the air intake of the carburetor.

Percolation: A form of vapor lock in which gas in the lines ''boils'', or percolates, from excessive heat.

Ping: See ignition.

Pinion: The smaller of two gears in mesh.

Piston: A tightly fitted cylindrical shaped piece of metal that slides up and down inside the cylinder and imparts the driving force to the connecting rod and crankshaft by the pressure of the burning fuel/air charge.

Piston pin: One of the thin, narrow bands of metal that are contained in grooves around the periphery of the piston. The piston ring acts as a bearing between the piston and cylinder wall and helps to seal in the burning charge during combustion.

Pitman arm: A connecting arm between the steering box and the steering linkage of the front wheels.

Plate: Lead-or lead-peroxide grids in the battery that, together with the electrolytic solution, generate electricity.

Points: The set of contacts in the distributor that separate to produce a spark, or surge of current, at the electrodes of the spark plug.

Polarity: The manner, or direction, in which electricity flows.

Post: One of the two protuberances on either end of the battery on which the battery cables are attached. The positive post is the thicker of the two posts.

Power brakes: Brakes that have a power assist to lessen the amount of pressure needed to apply the brakes.

Power steering: Steering system in which an engine-driven pump reduces the effort needed to turn the steering wheel.

Power stroke: The third of the four strokes in an engine's operating cycle that takes place when the energy of the burning fuel/air charge exerts pressure against the piston to drive it down the cylinder.

Pre-ignition: A form of ignition that occurs before normal ignition by the spark plug. Pre-ignition can be caused by "hot spots" inside the combustion chamber, such as carbon deposits or an overheated spark plug.

164

Pressure plate: A component in the clutch assembly that pushes the clutch disc against the engine's flywheel to connect the engine drive up with the transmission.

Pressure relief valve: A valve, such as incorporated in the oil-pump unit, to relieve excessive pressure of the oil being pumped.

Primary circuit: Low-voltage-circuit system that consists of the battery, primary-coil windings, points and condenser, and ignition switch.

Primary shoe: One of the shoes in a conventional drum-brake design that has the greater retarding effect on the drum, when the brakes are applied.

Propeller shaft: Another term for the driveshaft.

Pumpkin: A common term for the differential housing in the rear end.

R

Radial-ply tire: A type of tire construction in which the cord fibers in the plies are arranged at right angles to the beads.

Radiator: The "honeycomb" container of coolant, located in the front of the car, which dissipates the heat picked up by the coolant from the engine.

Radiator cap: The cap located on top of the radiator.

Reach: The length of a spark plug's threaded portion of its shell that screws into the head.

Rear axle: Part of a car driveline on which the rear wheels are located.

Rear suspension: Consists of the rear axle shock absorbers and coil leaf-spring assembly.

Reservoir: A part of the engine or one of the components in which a fluid is stored.

Resistance: A measure of the difficulty a wire or some other electrical component offers to the flow of electricity.

Resistor: Some part of the electrical system, such as a piece of special high-resistance wire, which is designed to set up a certain amount of resistance to the flow of current in a system.

Resonator: An auxiliary muffler often found on luxury cars. Its purpose is to provide additional muffling of the exhaust gases.

Retracting springs: A spring or springs that pulls rather than pushes. Used on choke, throttle linkage, clutch, brakes, hood counter-balance mechanism, etc.

Rim: The outer circumference of a wheel on which the tire is mounted.

Ring gear: Ring-shaped gear with teeth on its side, located in differential housing; the ring gear provides the motive power for the rear-axle assembly and wheels.

Rocker arm: Finger-shaped component that pivots on a shaft to open the intake and exhaust valve in the combustion chamber.

Rotor: Term for either the disc on which the brake pads press against or the part of the distributor that directs current from the coil to the spark plugs.

Run out: The degree of wobble which a wheel has when it turns.

Rust inhibitor: A chemical added to the coolant in the radiator to coat the inside areas of the cooling system to minimize rust of the metal surfaces.

S

Safety rim: A wheel rim that is humped on its inner edge, where the tire bead seats, to keep the tire from coming off the rim in the event of a blowout.

Seal: A flexible material between two hard surfaces usually intended to keep some sort of fluid in its place.

Although this scratch on a rotor looks harmless enough, it can divert the high-tension current and prevent an engine from starting. You have to look closely to spot one of these "carbon tracks".

Secondary circuit: The circuit in the ignition system that produces the high voltage to fire the spark plugs. It consists of the secondary windings in the coil, the high-tension wire between the coil and distributor, the distributor cap and rotor, and the spark plugs and their cables.

Separator: A partition between the negative and positive plates in a battery to keep them from touching each other and short-circuiting.

Shackle: A pivoting support for one end of a leaf spring that attaches the spring to the frame.

Shock absorber: A telescoping component that absorbs the impact forces from the tire and wheel assembly.

Slip joint: A hollow, splined shaft that slides over the transmission output shaft or the axle shaft to accomodate changes in length, as the shaft(s) move up or down.

167

Sludge: A dirty, thickened oil.

Snap ring: A c-shaped piece of wire of flat, springy steel that locks a component in place on a shaft, such as the piston pin that is kept in place in the piston.

Solenoid: An electromagnetic switching device. It consists of an iron core surrounded by a coil of wire that moves due to the magnetic attraction induced when current is fed to the coil.

On modern cars, idle speed is set with the idle-speed solenoid (arrow). The length of the plunger that pushes against the throttle linkage is adjusted by either adjusting a screw on the solenoid or by loosening a locknut and turning the solenoid itself.

168

Spark plug: The final link in the secondary circuit, the spark plug screws into the combustion chamber. Current flows through the center electrode and jumps a gap to the ground electrode to ignite the air/gas charge.

Specific gravity: The density or weight, of a fluid as compared with water.

Spider gears: The gears inside the differential that allow the inside wheel and axle to turn at a slower speed than the outside wheel and axle to prevent damage to the axles.

Spindle: The stubby front axle.

Splines: Gear-like notches on a shaft that engage other notches inside another component to make a very secure joint.

Spring: One of the suspension members that supports the car and isolates impact forces from the road surface.

Sprocket: A gear-like component that has its outer circumference notched so that it can transfer its rotational movement to another sprocket by way of a notched belt or chain.

Stabilizer bar: A bar or rod that braces the car's suspension so that it becomes more stable during certain driving conditions, as when cornering.

Starting system: Comprised of the battery and its cables, the starter, the solenoid, the ignition switch and the neutral-safety switch.

Steering column: The shaft on which the steering wheel is connected.

Steering linkage: Various rods, arms and other linkage that transfers the motion of the pitman arm to the front wheels.

Stroke: The distance that the piston moves up or down in its cylinder.

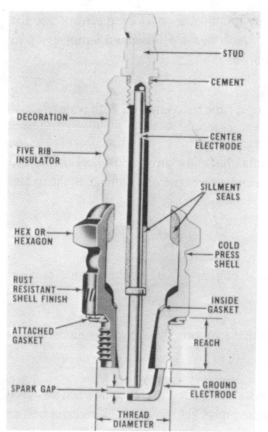

STUD

CEMENT

DECORATION

CENTER
ELECTRODE

FIVE RIB
INSULATOR

SILLMENT
SEALS

HEX OR
HEXAGON

COLD
PRESS
SHELL

RUST
RESISTANT
SHELL FINISH

INSIDE
GASKET

ATTACHED
GASKET

REACH

SPARK GAP

GROUND
ELECTRODE

THREAD
DIAMETER

Components in the secondary ignition system.
(Courtesy Champion)

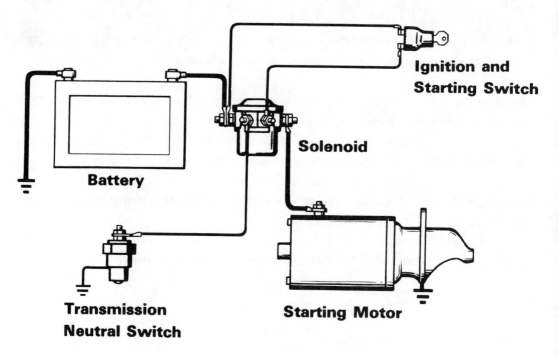

Ignition and
Starting Switch

Solenoid

Battery

Transmission
Neutral Switch

Starting Motor

Suspension system: Includes all the pieces that support the vehicle on its axles or wheels. Those members are the springs, shock absorbers, control arms, torsion bar, stabilizer bar, and their connecting parts to the frame.

Support bearing: A bearing that has the job of holding a shaft in place, such as a crankshaft main bearing.

T

Tachometer: An instrument used to measure engine speed or rpm.

Tailpipe: The last section of exhaust piping that connects to the muffler and extends to the rear of the vehicle.

Temperature gauge: An instrument that measures the temperature of a fluid or coolant, such as the radiator coolant.

Terminal: A point of connection.

Test light: A small light that, when hooked up with wires to a complete electrical circuit, will glow. The test light is used to locate short circuits in an electrical system.

Thermostat: A temperature sensitive switch.

Throttle-stop modulator: Another term for idle-speed solenoid, the device that keeps the throttle from closing completely at idle speeds.

Throwout bearing: Bearing in the clutch. A lever moves the bearing back and forth as the clutch pedal is operated, to engage and disengage the clutch.

Tie Rod: One of the rods by which motion from the pitman arm is transmitted to the front wheel.

Timing chain: A chain that links up the motion of the crankshaft to the camshaft by means of sprockets.

171

Timing light: A stroboscopic light that is flashed according to the pulsations of current to the spark plug. The timing light is used to check the ignition timing of an engine.

Tire pressure: The amount of air pressure in a tire. It's measured in pounds per square inch (psi).

Toe-in: A dimension that describes the degree that the front of the front wheels point toward each other.

Toe-out: The opposite of toe in; a condition in which the front wheels point away from each other.

Torque converter: The part of an automatic transmission responsible for converting or transferring motion from the engine to the transmission through a fluid medium.

Troubleshoot: A term that describes the procedure or procedures for systematically tracking down the cause for a malfunction in a component or system.

Tubeless tire: A tire that doesn't contain an inner tube.

U

U-bolt: A U-shaped clamp used for holding exhaust pipes and mufflers in place.

Universal joint: Also called a U-joint. It is a flexible link in the driveshaft. A U-joint makes allowances for the up-and-down movement of the driveshaft assembly as the car's suspension absorbs impact forces.

V

Vacuum advance: A vacuum-operated level that advances and retards the spark, or ignition timing, according to the speed of the engine.

172

Valve train: Describes all the members having to do with the operation of the valves: pushrods, valves and springs, rocker arms, and cam followers or tappets.

Vapor lock: A condition that occurs when a fuel line absorbs so much heat that it vaporizes the gasoline and obstructs the flow of fuel.

Vent: Small orifice in the fuel tank, carburetor, or some other component that permits air to enter and prevent a vacuum from forming.

Venturi: A narrow passage in the carburetor throat that speeds up the flow of air and causes a pressure drop, so that gas can be withdrawn from the float bowl and atomized.

Voltage: A unit of measurement of electrical current. Pertains to the pressure needed or available to make current flow.

Voltage regulator: An electrical device that controls the amount of current produced by the alternator or generator. It also acts as a cutoff device for preventing battery current from draining back through the system when the engine is idling or shut off.

Viscosity: A term that is an indication of the "thickness" or body of a fluid. A heavy viscosity oil has a high degree of resistance to flow.

W

Water jacket: A hollow passage surrounding the cylinder. Coolant flows through the water jackets and carries heat back to the radiator.

Water pump: Forces coolant throughout the engine, hoses, and radiator. The water pump is driven by a fan belt from the crankshaft pulley.

Wheel balancing: Making symetric the dynamic force created by the weight of a spinning wheel. Special weights are placed on the outer circumference of the wheel or rim to correct any imbalance.

173

Wheel bearing: Load bearing friction reducing ring on the axle end. It permits a wheel to turn with a minimum of friction.

Wheel cylinder: A slave sylinder located on a wheel's backing plate that presses the linings into contact with the brake drums.

Wheel well: The underside of a fender directly over the wheel itself.

Wingnut: A nut that has ''ears'' so that it can be turned by hand. The carburetor air-cleaner housing is usually secured with a wingnut. Wingnuts are used wherever quick, frequent and easy removal is anticipated.

Wire gauge: A wire of uniform, precise thickness used to measure the gap between the electrodes on a spark plug.

Z

Zerk fitting: A grease fitting. It consists of a small plug with an orifice to admit grease. Inside is a ball-check valve that keeps the grease from leaking back out through the orifice.

Mechanical Maintenance Schedule*

SERVICES SCHEDULED BY ACCUMULATED MILEAGE

ODOMETER READING IN THOUSANDS	5	10, 20, 25, 35, 40, 50, 55, 65, 70, 80, 85, 95, 100	15, 45, 75	30, 60, 90
Engine Oil, Oil Filter and Fluids (Chart 1)	●	●	●	●
Complete Body Lubrication & Brake Inspection (Chart 2)			●	●
Front Suspension and Steering - Verify condition/action and *correct as required*			●	●
Manual Transmission Clutch — inspect/correct adjustment			●	●
Complete Chassis Lubrication (Chart 3)				●
U.S. EMISSION CONTROL SERVICES — Idle Speed (curb and fast) — check/correct	●			
Complete precision tune-up (Chart 4)				●
Fuel Filter — Replace			●	
Drive Belts — Inspect condition and tension, or *replace as required*	●		●	

CHART 1
Engine Oil, Oil Filter and Fluids — Every 5,000 Miles

Engine Oil and Oil Filter

Change required every 5,000 miles or 5 months, whichever comes first. If most car uses involve trips under 6 miles, change oil once between the oil and filter changes. Check engine oil level every 500 to 600 miles.

Fluids

Inspect and correct levels in battery, transmission (and overdrive where applicable), cooling system, power steering reservoir, manual steering gear, master cylinder, windshield washer and rear axle. Add fluid as required.

CHART 2
Complete Body Lubrication and Brake Inspection — Every 15,000 Miles

Brake Inspection

Inspect linings and other parts of brake system. Adjust, lubricate, and *correct as required*
Parking Brake — adjust as required

Body Lubrication

Apply silicone lubricant to all door, window and trunk (or tailgate) rubber weather seals
Ash tray slides
Courtesy light switch buttons
Door latches, lock cylinders and door hinges
Front seat tracks
Glove box door latch and hinge
Hood latch and hinges
Trunk lid or tailgate hinges and latches

CHART 3
Complete Chassis Lubrication — Every 30,000 Miles

Inspection and Lubrication

Clutch levers and linkage
Front suspension ball joints (with replacement of suspension and steering system seals as required)
Front wheel bearings
Rear axle (change lubricant)
Turning radius stop

NOTE: Universal joints and rear wheel bearings do not require periodic or scheduled lubrication

---

SERVICES SCHEDULED BY MILEAGE OR TIME INTERVALS

AUTOMATIC TRANSMISSION

For cars in normal use, no maintenance is required except fluid checks. For cars in heavy-duty use and service, change fluid and filter and adjust bands every 30,000 miles or 30 months, whichever comes first.

ENGINE COOLANT

Charge required at 25,000 miles or 25 months, whichever comes first, and then at the start of every winter season.

TIRES

Tires and tire services are excluded from both the New Car Guarantee and this Maintenance schedule Tire adjustments are handed directly by their manufacturers. Their normal maintenance recommendations appear as guides under "Tire Condition" in this Technical Service Manual.

BATTERY CABLES

Inspect and clean at the start of every winter season.

CHART 4
Complete Precision Tune-Up — Every 30,000 Miles

A precision electronic diagnosis should be purchased whenever questionable engine performance occurs between the scheduled complete precision tune-ups.

Air-Guard System Hoses — inspect and *correct as required*
Carburetor Air Cleaner Element — replace
Choke Linkage — inspect for free movement *(correct as required)*
Coil and Spark Plug Wires — inspect and *replace as required*
Distributor Advance Mechanisms — check and *correct as required*
Distributor Cap and Rotor — inspect and *replace as required*
*Drive Belts — inspect condition and tighten or *correct as required*
Engine oil Filler Cap (filter type) — clean and soak in oil
Fuel Filter Element — replace
Fuel System, Cap, Tank, Lines and Connections — inspect for integrity and *correct as required*
Fuel Vapor Inlet Filter at Charcoal Canister — replace
Heat Valve (exhaust manifold) — inspect and lubricate
Idle Speed (curb and fast) and mixture — check and reset as required
Ignition Timing — check and set as required
PCV Filter (6-cylinder) — clean
PCV Hoses — inspect and *replace as required*
PCV Valve — replace
Spark Plugs — replace
TAC System Hoses — inspect and *correct as required*
Transmission Controlled Spark System — inspect and *correct as required*
Vaccuum Fittings, Hoses and Connections — inspect and *correct as required*

*During extended high temperature and extensive air conditioner operation the drive belts may require more frequent inspection and adjustment

---

* NOTE: *This Mechanical Maintenance Schedule identifies all required services by mileage or time intervals. It is the owner's responsibility to have the services performed — and to pay for them.*

Services listed above and followed by the words "as required" (in italic type) may be necessary if a system is found to be defective or maladjusted. These "as required" services are also the owner's responsibility — except if performed within the new car guarantee period.

5/78